A Grammar Course for TEFL Certificate

Tony Penston

tp   TP Publications

Published by TP Publications
59 Applewood Heights
Greystones
Co. Wicklow
Ireland

© Tony Penston 1998

First published 1998

ISBN 0 9531323 0 7

Cover artwork by Kevin Brooks

Printed by Enprint
Earl's Court Industrial Estate
Dublin 14

CONTENTS

Acknowledgements, Thanks .... *iv*

Introduction .... *v*

Abbreviations and symbols .... *vi*

1. The Simple Sentence and its Parts 1

2. Verb Tenses 11

3. The Present Perfect 26

4. Nouns 27

5. Quantifiers 29

6. Pronouns.. 31

7. Adjectives 32

8. Adverbs... 34

9. Degrees of Comparison 36

10. The Passive Voice 38

11. Irregular Verbs 40

12. Modal Auxiliary Verbs 41

13. Phrasal Verbs 43

14. Questions 44

15. Clauses 45

16. Reported Speech 47

17. Relative Clauses 50

18. Conditionals 52

19. Infinitive and *-ing* Form 56

20. Negation 58

21. Discourse Markers 59

22. The Articles 60

23. Recognition Test 61

24. Error Analysis 62

Answers to tasks *66*

Index *72*

Acknowledgements

We are grateful to the following for permission to reproduce copyright material (abbreviations of publishers' names used in captions are included; coursebooks are student's book editions):

•Addison Wesley Longman Ltd. (Longman) for extracts from *New Blueprint Intermediate* by B. Abbs & I. Freebairn (1995), *Teaching Tenses* by R. Aitken (1992), *Advanced Communication Games* by J. Hadfield (1987) and *Intermediate Matters* by J. Bell & R. Gower (1991). •Cambridge University Press (CUP) for extracts from *New Cambridge English 1* by M. Swan & C. Walter (1990), *Cambridge English for Schools Student's Book One* by A. Littlejohn & D. Hicks (1996), *English Grammar in Use* by R. Murphy (1994), *English Vocabulary in Use - Pre-intermediate & Intermediate* by S. Redman (1997), *Language in Use - Pre-intermediate, Language in Use - Intermediate* and *Language in Use - Upper-intermediate* by A. Doff & C. Jones (1991, 94 & 97) and *Grammar Practice Activities* by P. Ur (1988). •Heinemann Educational Publishers, a division of Reed Educational & Professional Publishing Ltd. (Heinemann) for an extract from *Grammar Activities 1* by W. Forsyth & S. Lavender (1995) and *Reward - Elementary* by S. Greenall (1997). •Oxford University Press (OUP) for extracts from *Lifelines Pre Intermediate* by T. Hutchinson (1997), *New First Certificate Masterclass* by S. Haines & B. Stewart (1996), *Business Objectives* by and © V. Hollett (1996), *New Headway Intermediate* by L. & J. Soars (1996) and *OK4* by D. Bolton et al (1990). •Penguin Books Ltd. (Penguin) for an extract from *Grammar Games and Activities* by P. Watcyn-Jones (1995). •Prentice Hall Europe (PH) for an extract from *Making Sense of Phrasal Verbs* by M. Shovel (1992).

We are grateful to the following for permission to reproduce photographs (on page 37):

Frank Spooner Picture Stills (Laurel & Hardy); Ronald Grant Picture Library (Tom & Jerry); Collections (fisherman); Network Photographers (D.J.).

References

Books I have referred to include *Practical English Usage* by M. Swan (Oxford University Press 1995), *A Practical English Grammar* by A.J. Thomson & A.V. Martinet (Oxford University Press 1986), *A Student's Grammar of English* by R. Quirk & S. Greenbaum (Longman 1990), *A Communicative Grammar of English* by G. Leech & J. Svartvik (Longman 1994), *Syntactic Theory and the Structure of English* by A. Radford (Cambridge University Press 1997), *Discover English* by R. Bolitho & B. Tomlinson (Heinemann 1995), *Teaching Tenses* by R. Aitken (Longman 1992), *Oxford Advanced Learner's Dictionary, COBUILD Dictionary*, and *Webster's Collegiate Dictionary, Tenth Edition.*

Thanks

To Tim Graham at Sheffield Hallam University (Trinity College London TESOL Course), Cathy Gannon at University College, Cork (RSA/Cambridge CELTA Course), Moira Prendergast at Regional Technical College, Waterford (WRTC TEFL Course), Linda Hickey at Language and Leisure Ireland, Dublin (RELSA TEFL Course) and Greg Rosenstock at Bluefeather School of Languages, Dublin (ATT TEFL Course) for their valuable feedback and support.

To Anne Kelly for her assistance with the wordprocessing.

And Patricia O'Neill for logistical back-up.

Not forgetting my students and trainees over the years, who are still educating me.

Introduction

This book has been written in order to provide a course in grammar for native speaker participants on a TEFL certificate course (English language teachers in training). There are good grammar books already available for use in ELT, but most are reference books and/or are addressed more to the language student than the teacher, and therefore do not lend themselves to continuous coursework in a training environment.

Native English speakers in their early years of teaching often find themselves at a loss to explain some of the structures of their own language. Blame for this may be placed on an extreme view of the communicative approach to language teaching, i.e. communication alone is sufficient for good language teaching/learning. Indeed it used to be understood that the novice native-speaking teacher would expand and polish her knowledge of the grammar as she followed the coursebook class by class, but with more and more emphasis on authentic materials, games, projects, etc, the teacher now has to operate with more unpredictable language in the classroom. Today's language learner is sophisticated and demands both communicative activities *and* competent grammar explanation.

The need for well-balanced training courses is obvious. For those course directors and tutors who require structured material for a grammar component suited to a certificate course, this book should prove helpful.

Again, this book is primarily a coursebook, and should be read chapter by chapter, as later chapters presume a reading of earlier ones. However, a user-friendly index is included which will enable the teacher to use this book also as a basic grammar reference.

In the early stages I have made an effort to avoid overloading with difficult language, so allowance should be made for the occasional simplistic definition, e.g. the subject of a sentence being the 'doer', etc.

Where the matching tasks are used in class, the tutor should cut out, mount and laminate the sections for group/pair work where possible. The tutor may also project the task and answer on the overhead projector. Copyright is waived for such tutor activities but I would stress that in order to comply with copyright legislation *each course participant should also have a copy of this book.*

It must be stressed that the activities in this book are designed for *teachers*, not for language *students*. The copious extracts from EFL coursebooks contained within are intended to show the difference between what the teacher should know and what and how she should teach.

On completion of *A Grammar Course for TEFL Certificate* the English language teacher should have a well-ordered knowledge of the basics of English grammar, with the confidence this brings and shows in her classwork. This cannot be acquired from dipping into general grammar books or collating various handouts.

I would here like to include a few points on what I believe an English language teacher should know about grammar and its teaching:

1. The teacher should know **the terminology**, for at least two reasons: (a) it is probable that her students will use grammatical terms when asking questions about a structure, (b) it is very difficult to explain a grammar rule without knowing the names of the items affected by that rule, e.g. how do you explain *If I had had ...* without knowing the terms *auxiliary* and *main/lexical verb*, even *past participle*?

2. The teacher should know **the structure rules**, because this is perhaps the most essential part of a language, and clear explanation should be available to the student on request. Position and function of adverbs, inversion of subject and auxiliary, choice of relative pronoun ... information on any of these and more may be requested without advance notice.

3. The teacher should know **how to fit the semantic (meaning) with the grammatical**, i.e. we don't just explain the *what* of the structure, but also the *why,* the use/function of the structure. For example, it would be inadvisable to devote much class time to explaining the structure of the passive voice or organizing exercises which require students to transform active sentences into passive and vice versa. The good teacher knows how to teach the 'feeling' for the passive and not to have students produce language of questionable communicative value.

4. The teacher should know **when to teach grammar**, better said, *exploit* grammar to aid the learning of the language. This involves knowing whether her students are the type who use grammar as a 'mental framework' for language acquisition or not (this sounds abstract but this type is evidenced by constant questioning about grammatical points, and is often consequently accused of testing the teacher). The *when* also refers to order of presentation - it is usually better for the learner to observe and use a new piece of language in a communicative context before the relevant grammar is introduced overtly, *if such is required.*

5. The teacher should know **when not to teach grammar**, that is, not to present grammar for grammar's sake. Primarily the teacher is a teacher of English communication, not of English grammar, and these in effect are two different subjects, evidenced by the fact that native speakers never had to learn (consciously) the grammar of their own language in order to communicate.

6. The teacher should know **how much grammar to teach** at each level. Most experienced teachers know when to tell a white lie in order to keep information simple and not overwhelm slow learners or learners at lower levels. For instance, at beginner level the student need not know that there is more than one time reference for the present continuous tense.

This book should go some way towards providing the skills outlined in the points above, especially points 1-3. The latter three may require practical guidance.

Remarks and suggestions from users of this book would be greatly appreciated.

Abbreviations

adj	adjective	L1	first/native language, mother tongue
adv	adverb	L2	second/foreign/target language
AmE	American English	noun/-phrase	noun or noun phrase
aux	auxiliary verb	pro, prep	pronoun, preposition
BrE	British English	SUBJ	subject
def/indef art	definite/indefinite article	T	task/teacher
IrE	Irish English	verb/-phrase	verb or verb phrase
TEFL/ELT	Teaching English as a Foreign or Second Language / English Language Teaching		

Symbols

*	Asterisk at start of sentence indicates it is ungrammatical.
?	Question mark at start of sentence indicates it is semantically obscure.
( )° ... ( )°	Only one of the parenthesized items may occur in the sentence.

1   The Simple Sentence and its Parts

A tree diagram (branching downwards) serves well to show the constituents of a sentence:

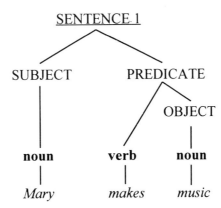

Sentence 1 shows us that a sentence must have two main branches (constituents): the **subject** and the **predicate**. The subject is usually the 'doer', or the person/thing described. The predicate simply means 'the rest of the sentence'.

The **verb** conveys an action or state. The **object** is the person/thing at the receiving end of the action, hence *music* is the object of the verb *makes*. The verb and object are contained within the predicate.

In every sentence there must be a **finite verb**, i.e. a verb with a tense. A verb can change its form to show tense, e.g. *show : showed*. The verb in sentence 1 is in the present tense. Tenses are dealt with in the next chapter.

---

subject: the 'doer', or where there's no action, the person/thing considered.
predicate: the rest of the sentence after the subject.
verb: conveys an action or state, e.g. *to carry, to be*.
object: the person/thing at the receiving end of the action.
finite verb: a verb with a tense.

In sentence 1 the subject and object are **nouns**. They could be **pronouns**: *She makes it*. Pronouns are dealt with in more detail later.

---

noun: a person, place or thing, e.g. *Mary, Athens, bike*.
pronoun: a word standing for (pro) a noun.

Some sentences consist of only one word, e.g. the imperative *Stop!*, but then the missing part is understood and we can usually construct what we call an underlying sentence. In this case the underlying sentence is something like *You (will) stop*.

Many words can function as either nouns or verbs. Two words in the list below cannot serve this dual function. Which are they?

spoon	serve	wait	compost	rile	keep
meet	sloop	convict	effect	remove	settle

Note: It is advisable to have a dictionary to hand when using this book. Popular EFL dictionaries include the *Oxford Advanced Learner's Dictionary*, the *Longman Dictionary of Contemporary English*, the *Collins COBUILD English Dictionary* and the *Cambridge International Dictionary of English*.

Our second sentence doesn't have any object:

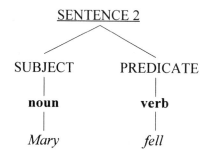

SENTENCE 2

SUBJECT   PREDICATE

noun   **verb**

Mary   *fell*

Now compare sentences 1 and 2:

In sentence 1 the verb *to make* must have an object. We can't just say *Mary makes*. Our listener would say *Mary makes what?*. Verbs that must take an object are called **transitive verbs**. Other transitive verbs are *to have, to afford*, etc.

In sentence 2 there is no object. Mary didn't fall her body, didn't fall the clarinet, etc. The verb *to fall* can't take an object; it is an intransitive verb. Other intransitive verbs are *to cough, to hesitate*, etc.

> **transitive verb:** a verb that must take an object.
> **intransitive verb:** a verb that cannot take an object.

Some verbs may be used transitively or intransitively:
  Mary sings ballads. (transitive)
  Mary sings. (intransitive)

T1.2

Most of the verbs in the list below can be used transitively or intransitively. However, two can only be used transitively and two only intransitively. Which are they?

follow	escape	reflect	pass	decline	prosper
kneel	fit	respect	count	discover	loop

Now observe sentence 3:

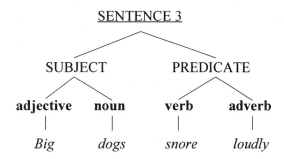

SENTENCE 3

SUBJECT — PREDICATE

adjective — noun — verb — adverb

Big — dogs — snore — loudly

Sentence 3 reminds us that adjectives mostly come *before* the noun, and adverbs of manner will often *follow* the verb (or verb + object). The syntax in **Dogs big loudly snore* may be okay in many languages but not in English (an asterisk at the start of a sentence or phrase signifies it is ungrammatical).

> **adjective:** a word that gives information about a noun.
> **adverb of manner:** a word that gives information about a verb.

Moving along now to the next sentence:

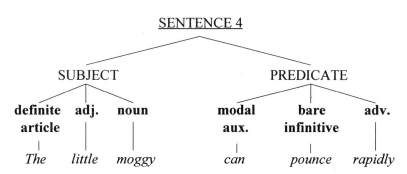

SENTENCE 4

SUBJECT — PREDICATE

definite article — adj. — noun — modal aux. — bare infinitive — adv.

The — little — moggy — can — pounce — rapidly

In sentence 4 we are introduced to the **definite article**, the **modal auxiliary verb** (shortened to *modal aux.*, *modal verb*, even simply *modal*, or for students, *help verb*), and the **infinitive**.

The citation form of verbs, e.g. *to swim, to afford, to snore*, is the infinitive, or to be more precise, the **infinitive with** *to*.

Modal aux. verbs, e.g. *may, might, can, could, would*, etc, are followed by the base form of the main verb, more commonly called the **infinitive without** *to* or the **bare infinitive**.

The imperative (order) also uses the bare infinitive, e.g. <u>*Strike while the iron's hot.*</u>

> **definite article:** *the*, indicating the known or unique.
> **indefinite article:** *a, an*, indicating the not known/the not unique/any one.
> **modal aux. verb:** *can, could, may, might, will, would, shall, should, must, ought to*.
> Modals indicate probability, permission, advice, etc.
> **infinitive:** base form of the verb, with or without *to*. It has no tense.

T1.3 Draw a tree diagram for the sentence *A real man would shave closely*, using the term *bare infinitive* in the appropriate position.

In sentence 5 following we can see the indefinite article *a*, and the verb *be* (in the form of *was*) in its function of **primary auxiliary verb** (relax, there are only two types of aux. verb). In this instance the main verb takes the *-ing* form (pronounced 'ing' or I-N-G) and may be called the **-ing participle**. It is also known as the **present participle**, but this term is not user-friendly, having nothing to do with the present tense. Tenses are covered in the next chapter.

SENTENCE 5

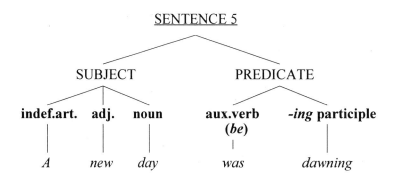

primary aux. verb:	*be, have,* and *do*. These can also act as main verbs. *Be* and *have* are not followed by the bare infinitive. Forms of *be* are: *am, are, is, were, was, being* and *been*.
***-ing* participle:**	form of main verb occurring after aux. verb *be* to form continuous aspect of tenses (see chapter 2).
main verb:	for TEFL purposes, the verb carrying the most 'sense', and occurring after the auxiliary verb. It is also called a lexical verb.

T1.4

Fill in your own text words at the bottom of the tree diagram below.

SENTENCE 6

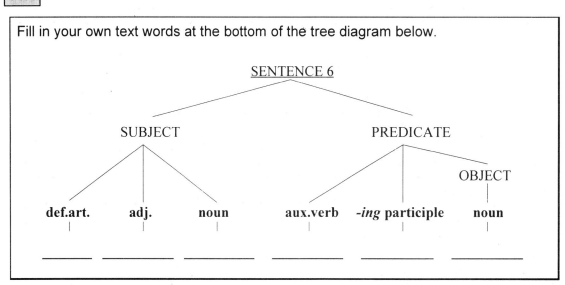

Fill in the two tree diagrams. Text words (in italics) follow, but choose wisely - three of these are redundant. The same text word cannot be used twice. Tip: fill in the text gaps first (line (c) in sentence 7 and line (d) in sentence 8). The text words are:

shock   a   the   might   Turkish   is   help   opening   audience   immensely   shall

SENTENCE 7

(a)   SUBJECT

(b)   _____   **noun**   _____   _____   _____

(c)   *An*   _____   *would*   _____   _____

SENTENCE 8

(a)   _____   PREDICATE

(b)

(c)   _____   **adj**   _____   **modal**   _____   _____   _____

(d)   *The*   _____   *play*   _____   _____   _____   _____

Fill in the blank columns below following the manner indicated in the first row.

EXAMPLE	WORD CLASS a)	WORD CLASS b)
*0. We reached **an** understanding .*	**pronoun**	*indefinite article*
*1. **Time** was **passing**.*		
*2. You **should** know **the** score.*		
*3. I **am** asking **them** to do it.*		
*4. Kiri can **sing** quite **beautifully**.*		
*5. **It** was a **rash** decision.*		

And now for another sentence:

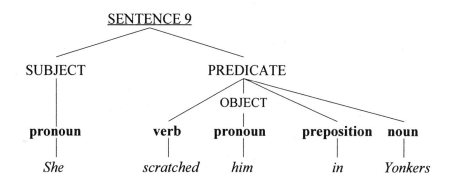

SENTENCE 9

```
                        SENTENCE 9
                   /                \
              SUBJECT              PREDICATE
                 |                  /       \
                 |              OBJECT
                 |              /    \
             pronoun      verb   pronoun   preposition   noun
                 |         |        |          |           |
               She     scratched   him         in        Yonkers
```

In sentence 9 we are introduced to (personal) **pronouns** and **prepositions**. You may notice that personal pronouns are the only words in English that have a different form for subject and object, i.e. sentence 9 is not *She scratched he*.

Observe the paradigm of personal pronouns below (the pronoun *it* may not often have personal reference but is included to complete the usual set):

PERSONAL PRONOUNS

	SUBJECT (NOMINATIVE CASE)		OBJECT (ACCUSATIVE CASE)	
	singular	plural	singular	plural
1st person	*I*	*we*	*me*	*us*
2nd person	*you*	*you*	*you*	*you*
3rd person	*she/he/it*	*they*	*her/him/it*	*them*

---

pronoun (revised):	a word which stands for a noun or noun phrase (see below), e.g. *he, it, they*; also indicating the communicators, *I, you*.
preposition:	many prepositions indicate location or direction, e.g. ***over** the moon*, ***to** the Louvre*; many others indicate time, e.g. ***in** July*, ***after** eight*; and then there is a 'mixed bag', e.g. ***for** me*, ***to** my surprise*, ***because of** him*, ***regarding** the divorce*, etc.

CARD 3

1 The sun went _____ a cloud.
2 Tunbridge Wells is _____ Hastings and London.
3 Do you go to work _____ car?
4 He broke his leg when he fell _____ the stairs.
5 What did you buy your mother_____ her birthday?

CARD 4

1 The children hid _____ the bed.
2 Shall I go with you _____ the station?
3 They bought a house _____ a very big garden.
4 Are you doing anything _____ the weekend?
5 She was born _____ December 10th.

From *Grammar Games and Activities* by P. Watcyn-Jones (Penguin). Prepositions bingo.

More on prepositions:

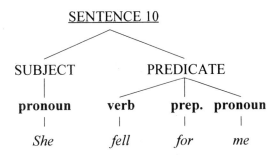

SENTENCE 10

SUBJECT   PREDICATE

pronoun   verb   prep.   pronoun

She   fell   for   me

Why is sentence 10 not *She fell for I? Because as you can see **prepositions take the object (accusative) case**. *Me* can't be the object of *fell*, because we know that *fall* is an intransitive verb. In a sentence such as *She sent him to me*, *him* is the object of the verb *send*, and *me* is the object of the preposition *to*.

---

a preposition(prep.) is always followed by a noun, noun phrase (see below) or pronoun in the object case (unless this has been moved out of normal position, e.g. *It was **me** she fell **for***).

Now that you have become acquainted with the term *case*, we should also include **word class** in our item list, although you have met this term before in Task 1.6. Word classes used to be, and still sometimes are, called **parts of speech**. Many linguists prefer the term *grammatical category*.

---

case: English has three cases: subject, object, and genitive (possessive).
word class: noun, verb, adjective, etc. Also called *part of speech* or *grammatical category*.

And we should also understand how words cluster into phrases. One which we mention here is the **noun phrase**. Briefly, a noun phrase is a group of words made up of a noun accompanied by one or more words qualifying or specifying it, e.g. *the curious didgeridoo*. In this book *noun/-phrase* means *noun or noun phrase*.

And now, what is the subject of the next sentence?

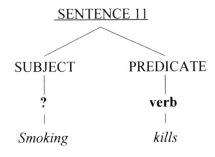

SENTENCE 11

SUBJECT   PREDICATE

?   verb

Smoking   kills

The word *smoking* comes from a verb, yet can take the place of a noun.

Besides being the subject in a sentence, the word *smoking* can occupy other noun positions, e.g.

> it can be the object of a verb: *She <u>likes smoking</u>;*
> it can follow a preposition: *We put it down <u>to smoking</u>;*
> and it can be preceded by a definite article: *It's <u>the smoking</u> that does it.*

This type of word is now tending to be called an **-*ing* noun**. It is also called a **gerund** or **verbal noun**.

There are a few nouns ending in *-ing* which do not have a verb counterpart, e.g. *shortening*. These should not be called *-ing nouns,* for the sake of distinction.

```
┌────────────────────────────────────────────────────────────────────┐
│   -ing noun: a word ending in -ing, derived from a verb, which can take the  │
│              place of a noun/-phrase. Also known as a gerund or verbal noun.  │
└────────────────────────────────────────────────────────────────────┘
```

```
┌──────┐    ┌──────────────────────────────────────────────┐
│ T1.7 │    │ Explain the error in                           │
└──────┘    │        *I look forward to see you.             │
            │ Use the terms preposition, -ing noun and infinitive. │
            └──────────────────────────────────────────────┘
```

Let us return to verbs. So far we have dealt only with verbs which convey or imply some activity. There is another type of verb worthy of attention:

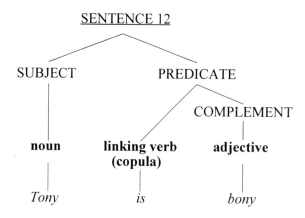

In sentence 12 the verb *be* is used as a main verb (its other role is an aux. verb - see sentence 5). As we can see, this verb does not take an object, as its job is just to describe things or people. It is called a **linking verb** (or *copula*) and it is followed by the **subject complement**.

```
┌────────────────────────────────────────────────────────────────────────┐
│ linking verb:      (also called copula or copular verb) a linking verb simply links the │
│                    subject with what is being said about it. Linking verbs comprise be  │
│                    and verbs of appearance, sense, etc, e.g. seem, feel, sound.         │
│ subject complement: an adjective, noun/-phrase, pronoun or adverbial linked to the subject │
│                    by a linking verb.                                    │
└────────────────────────────────────────────────────────────────────────┘
```

Fill in the blank columns below following the manner indicated in the first row.

EXAMPLE	WORD CLASS a)	WORD CLASS b)
0. We reached an understanding .	*pronoun*	*indefinite article*
1. I am rolling in it.		
2. Boots are for walking.		
3. They were looking at us.		
4. She seems very well to me.		
5. The proof of the pudding is in the eating.		
6. I will be seeing you.		
7. Stealthily the fox approached the old barn.		

T1.9

Fill in the two tree diagrams. Text words (in italics) follow, but choose carefully - two of these are redundant. The same text word cannot be used twice. Tip: fill in the text gaps in lines (c) first. Text words are:

noisy   good   quite   hell   him   gambling   the   to   discount   drove   sounds

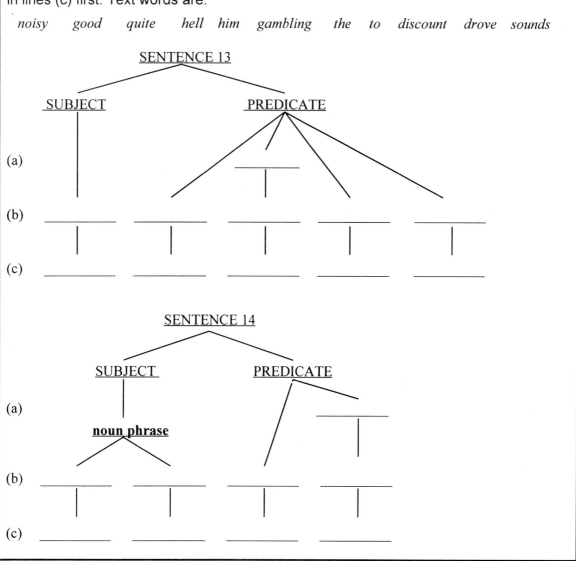

A NOTE ON TREE DIAGRAMS

Tree diagrams are used by most syntacticians to show the phrase structure of sentences, but there is not general conformity on the branching or applications. I have in this chapter compromised between traditional and modern terminology in order to present the material in a user-friendly way for English language teachers.

The division of a sentence into only two major constituents, subject and predicate, is not sacrosanct. In the case of adverbials (see chapter 8) which are not tied to the verb phrase* and commonly occur at the start or end of the sentence, there seems to be a strong case for a third major branch. Indeed, we can say that a sentence is composed of up to five major constituents: SUBJECT, VERB/-PHRASE, COMPLEMENT, OBJECT and ADVERBIAL.

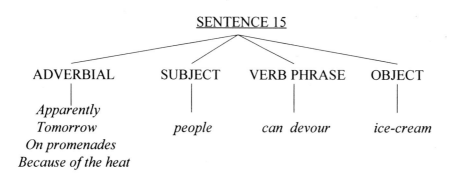

In the Classroom

Experience tells us that students with an Indo-European L1 have little difficulty in coping with the syntax of English. The case is often different for students whose L1 is of a non Indo-European family. Chinese students, for example, who are experiencing difficulty in correctly ordering constituent phrases or in conjoining clauses should benefit from the visual assistance the tree diagram provides.

However, as I reiterate throughout this book, **if they know it, don't teach it,** which means in this case if your students are able to communicate in reasonably well-structured sentences, or to acquire the rules of English sentence structure through normal communicative methodology then there's no need at all to teach sentence structure overtly.

And may I remind you that the material in this book is written for teachers, not for language learners. Please read the introduction for details

*A verb phrase, for our purposes, is made up of auxiliary verb(s) + main verb.

2 Verb Tenses

The method of presentation in this chapter partly follows NLP in that there is a storyline with seeing, hearing and feeling associations, and there are gentle revision sections. This should prevent 'overload', which is understandably experienced by many TEFL trainees when introduced to the English tense system.

2.1 PRESENT, PAST AND FUTURE TENSES

There are 3 tenses in English -   **present**
                                   past
                                   future

Each of these can be expanded to include certain aspects, as we will see below.

Our initial look at tenses will consist of a little story. It's a story about a girl in Sandymount who spends a lot of her time drawing. First, just read the story slowly. At this first reading there is no need to learn the titles of the tenses in parentheses - just look and move on.

TENSE SITUATIONS - EPISODE I

Deirdre Charcoal **draws** (PRESENT SIMPLE) for a living, which is handy, because she does almost nothing else but draw. As a matter of fact, at this very moment she **is drawing** (PRESENT CONTINUOUS) in her tudor style house near the screeching seagulls of Sandymount.

On a clear April evening in 1996 Deirdre saw a UFO land on Sandymount Strand and disgorge a gold-coloured alien. Deirdre sat on the granite wall and **drew** (PAST SIMPLE) this alien, who simply took a scoop of the wet sand, hopped back into the craft and flew off again. Deirdre reported the matter to the *Evening Echo* later that night. I was working as a reporter for the *Echo* at that time and I drove out to interview her the following morning.

Deirdre **was drawing** (PAST CONTINUOUS) home-brewed reddish wine from a cask when I arrived at her house. She splashed some of her creation into a glass for me. I found her wine better than her story. I didn't take her account seriously and my report was flippant. That same report, by the way, is to be included in a book entitled *Where Do They Get Them?*

When Deirdre finds out about the book she **will draw** (FUTURE SIMPLE) blood. However, the publishers of the book are not known for their lightning speed of work and by the time it is in the bookstores she **will be drawing** (FUTURE CONTINUOUS) the pension from some beeping pension-dispensing machine.

Episode 1 of Tense Situations introduces us to the three basic English tenses: PRESENT, PAST and FUTURE.

Note that the third person singular -*s* ending in the present simple (*I draw, you draw, he/she/it draws*) is an oddity and may not be acquired easily. Allow for slips, supply rich input, and time will look after the rest.

Table 1 below lists the three basic tenses, PRESENT, PAST and FUTURE, each with SIMPLE and CONTINUOUS aspect (see 2.3), and includes an example and brief statement of the use of each.

TENSE	EXAMPLE	USE
PRESENT SIMPLE	*She draws pictures.*	regular/habitual
PRESENT CONTINUOUS	*She is drawing pictures.*	happening now
PAST SIMPLE	*She drew an alien.*	past event (non-concurrent)
PAST CONTINUOUS	*She was drawing wine.*	concurrent* past event
FUTURE SIMPLE	*She will draw blood.*	prediction (non-concurrent event)
FUTURE CONTINUOUS	*She will be drawing the pension.*	prediction of concurrent event

Table 1. Present, past and future tenses. *See 2.3.1 and 2.3.2.

2.2 FORM AND FUNCTION OF TENSES

The **form** of a tense, i.e. what grammatical words and morphemes (parts of words) it is made up of, is dealt with in this book as the case arises. We already know from chapter 1 that in *A new day was dawning*, *was* is the verb *be* acting as an auxiliary verb, which contains the tense, here PAST, and *dawning* is an -ing participle. We now know that the *tense* formed in this way is the **past continuous**.

By **function(s)** of a tense we mean what it is used for in communication. I prefer the term USE (see table 1), to avoid conflict with **language functions** in ELT syllabuses (e.g. asking for information, expressing likes/dislikes, giving instructions, etc.), which are not systematically related to grammar.

For simplicity' sake the uses in table 1 are restricted. More uses are included later.

2.3 ASPECT

The terms *simple* and *continuous* (and later, *perfect*) are known as **aspects**. In many grammar books the term *progressive* is used instead of continuous, but teachers seem to prefer the latter. The full title of the tense in *She is drawing now* is actually PRESENT TENSE, CONTINUOUS ASPECT, but most teachers say PRESENT CONTINUOUS TENSE, as this is less cumbersome.

2.3.1 Explaining the continuous aspect
The use of the continuous aspect is difficult to explain briefly. Many teachers have been accused of over-simplifying by stating that the continuous aspect conveys continuity. This is of course incomplete, but for many students at lower levels it suffices, so long as contextual and visual helps (see 2.5) are offered to illustrate other essential uses such as, in the past tense, to show that the event is concurrent with or interrupted by another.

2.3.2 Note on terminology
The word *concurrent* is used in the tables to cover, besides its usual meaning, the focus on *action in progress* or *temporary state* use of the continuous aspect. A [1] point of time or [2] duration is usually supplied in context:
[1] *At five o'clock? I was washing the cranberries.*
[2] *We were discussing Humanism all morning.*

If the concept of *concurrent* is causing problems, you might try replacing this term with the simplistic *continuous* wherever it appears (subject to tutor approval where applicable). Note, by the way, that the term *concurrent* is not intended for general use in the EFL classroom.

2.4 REVIEW PRESENT, PAST AND FUTURE TENSES

Now read the abridged version of episode 1 of *Tense Situations*, and this time pay attention to all the words in bold type-face.

> Deirdre Charcoal **draws (PRESENT SIMPLE)** quite a lot, indoors and out.
> I'm sure she **is drawing (PRESENT CONTINUOUS)** now, near the seagulls.
>
> In 1996 she **drew (PAST SIMPLE)** a golden alien on Sandymount Strand.
> She **was drawing (PAST CONTINUOUS)** red wine when I knocked on her door.
>
> She **will draw (FUTURE SIMPLE)** blood when she hears about the book.
> She **will be drawing (FUTURE CONTINUOUS)** the pension before then.

T2.1   Fill in the tenses in the right hand column below.

EXAMPLE	TENSE
1. She'll be coming round the mountain.	
2. I'm looking forward to that.	
3. I left my gallstone in San Francisco.	
4. We export our problems.	
5. She was thinking of going next week.	
6. You'll never walk a loan.	

2.5 THE TIME LINE

You may wish to use what is usually called a *time line* to illustrate problem tenses:

Figure 1. Time line for past simple and past continuous.

2.5.1 Visual value of the time line

Research shows that spoken explanation (auditory intake) alone can be insufficient if long-term memory retention is required. Time lines provide visual associations and certainly break the monotony of using only one medium. The one above shows how a single-action past activity (past simple) interrupts an ongoing one (past continuous). It may stop it completely, in which case the artwork would need just a little adjusting (the triangle would be a box blocking the end of the rectangle).

Please try to keep the blackboard neat for these visual helps - your picture may stay in your student's memory for many years. Write the word NOW, not PRESENT on the perpendicular (present time does not always equal present tense!). Try to use capital letters only for tense titles and other headings, and lowercase letters only for example sentences. Tense titles, however, are not usually necessary to include in time lines.

In my diagrams I use a box to 'enclose' a time reference. For simple aspect a large dot is used; for continuous aspect a wavy line is helpful. Boxes can be stretched to convey a specific time frame, so I prefer them to just lines intersecting the horizontal.

Try to give examples that are relevant or salient in some way - include topical events, students' names, your name, etc. And do remember the full stop at the end of a sentence.

Remember, like most grammar aids, the time line is mostly for use as a remedial help, i.e. when a student is experiencing some difficulty with tense usage. If there is no difficulty, move on. Don't bore the students with your fascinating knowledge!

2.6 PRESENT PERFECT TENSE

To continue our story:

TENSE SITUATIONS - EPISODE II

Deirdre **has entered** (PRESENT PERFECT SIMPLE) an art competition, which requires a submission of 50 still lifes of freckled bananas and green grapes.

She **has been working** (PRESENT PERFECT CONTINUOUS) hard for the last six weeks, sketching and shading, rubbing out and rubbing in, not to mention replacing the fruit as its colours change from those stipulated.

The two sentences in episode 2 of our story exemplify uses of the PRESENT TENSE, PERFECT ASPECT (subdivided into SIMPLE and CONTINUOUS aspects), or as we telescope it, the PRESENT PERFECT TENSE.

Please note in the story that although the *entering* and most if not all of the *working* occurred in the *past time* the tense is called *present* perfect. In case you have difficulty with this remember two things:
1. the auxiliary verb *have* is in the present tense, therefore we are dealing with the *present* perfect;
2. the focus of attention, or the consequence, is on the present, not the past.

N.B. The present perfect tense in English, unlike many European languages, does not allow mention of a past time (except with *since*), so concerned is it with the present. *Yesterday we have decided ...* is ungrammatical (as indicated by the prefixed asterisk). Even *This morning we have decided ...* is ungrammatical when the morning is over. In contrast, the past tense must be accompanied somewhere in the discourse by a reference to past time. This is a simple but important difference that is often overlooked in teaching.

The grammatical term *perfect* has little if any explanatory value in English now.

2.6.1 Form of the present perfect simple

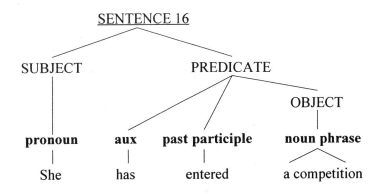

Please don't be distracted by the word *past* in *past participle*. The past participle can be used in any tense. For more detail on the aux. verb see 12.1.

> **past participle:** the third form of the verb, e.g.
> *broken* as in *break, broke, broken,* or
> *loved* as in *love, loved, loved*.

2.6.2 Uses of the present perfect simple

In the example in our story, *she has entered...*, you have only seen one use of the present perfect simple - **recent event** (relating to the present). There is one more important use - an **experience or achievement** anytime in one's life. An example of referring to experience/achievement would be *Deirdre has been to Peru*, or *Deirdre has had 7 near-death experiences.* You notice again we don't mention the past time as we are not concerned with it; what we are concerned with is *Deirdre*, in the present, through her experience. If we wish to shift the focus to the time of her experience, however, we must use the past tense, e.g. *When did she visit Peru?*

A time line can show the present perfect and past tense contrasted:

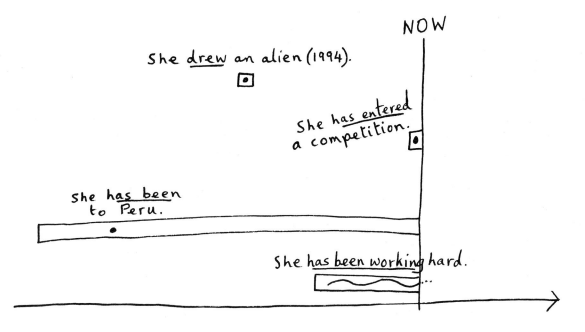

Figure 2. Time line for past simple and present perfect.

2.6.3 Form and use of the present perfect continuous

In the example *she has been working hard,* the first auxiliary, *has,* as usual, shows the tense. It is followed by the past participle of the second auxiliary *be,* then the main verb *work,* in the *-ing* participle form.

As for use, the present perfect continuous refers to an activity continuous up to now, which may or may not be completed. In the time line above the wavy line is continued with dots to imply that the activity is not yet completed (see also 2.14).

| T2.2 | Draw a time line to show the difference between *since* and *for* in *We've been working here since January/for four months.* |

And now to update our list of tenses to include the present perfect, simple (S.) and continuous (C.):

TENSE	EXAMPLE	USE
PRESENT SIMPLE	*She draws pictures.*	regular/habitual
PRESENT CONTINUOUS	*She is drawing pictures.*	happening now
PAST SIMPLE	*She drew an alien.*	past event (non-concurrent)
PAST CONTINUOUS	*She was drawing wine.*	concurrent past event
FUTURE SIMPLE	*She will draw blood.*	prediction (non-concurrent event)
FUTURE CONTINUOUS	*She will be drawing the pension.*	prediction of concurrent event
PRESENT PERFECT S.	*She has entered a competition.*	recent event or life experience
PRESENT PERFECT C.	*She has been drawing.*	continuous up to now

Table 2. Present, past, future, and present perfect tenses.

T2.3   Fill in the tenses in the right hand column below.

EXAMPLE	TENSE
1. I'll be with you now.	
2. I want it yesterday.	
3. He's seen the light.	
4. Are you joking?	
5. I wanted to know your name.	
6. You've been trying that all night.	
7. She'll be going up the wall.	
8. You weren't really listening.	

PRACTICE

1 Ask and answer about personal experiences, using the present perfect and the past simple of the verbs in the phrases below.

EXAMPLE
A: Have you ever been to the USA?
B: No, I haven't. Have you?
A: Yes, I went there with my parents two years ago.

1 go to the USA
2 break an arm or leg
3 see a famous person in real life
4 write to a magazine or newspaper
5 win a competition
6 find anything valuable

2 Look at the pictures. Ask and answer questions using the present perfect continuous.

EXAMPLE
1 A: What have you been reading?
   B: I've been reading a romantic novel.

1 What? 2 What? 3 What? 4 What? 5 Who?

3 In pairs, ask and say how long you have been doing the things in the list below. Use *for* or *since* in your answers.

1 living in your present home
2 studying in this school or college
3 learning English
4 using this textbook
5 doing this unit

4 Tell your partner about the following:

1 a sport or activity you've been doing a lot of recently
2 a sport you haven't done for a long time
3 a book you've been reading
4 a country you've always wanted to visit

🖳 LISTENING

Lori has written a letter to Glenn from Long Island in the USA and spoken it onto a cassette. Listen to her letter-cassette and say:

what annual event has just taken place.
what the weather's been like.
what happened to their summer cabin.
what she's been doing recently.

WRITING

Before you write

Look at the expressions below. You are writing an informal letter. Which would you use to: 1) start the letter 2) introduce a new topic 3) close the letter?

By the way, . . .
Did you know that . . .?
Thanks very much for your last letter.
Well, that's enough for now.
Sorry I haven't written before but . . .

It was great to get your letter.
Give my regards/love to . . .
Anyway, I'd better stop now.
Have you heard . . .?
Best wishes, . . .
Say hello to . . .
Love from . . .

Write a letter

Write to an English-speaking penfriend. Start by apologising for not writing before and give a reason. Describe some of the things you have done or have been doing recently. Say what the weather has been like. Close the letter by sending greetings to any other people you know.

From *New Blueprint Intermediate* by Abbs & Freebairn (Longman). Practising present perfect (simple and continuous) and past simple.

2.7 PAST PERFECT TENSE

To continue our story:

TENSE SITUATIONS - EPISODE III

I realize I was rather heartless with Deirdre at the interview. After all, she **had drawn** (PAST PERFECT SIMPLE) some extra sketches of the golden alien for the newspaper earlier that morning, sketches which were unfortunately below par as she **had been drinking** (PAST PERFECT CONTINUOUS) her brew between the strokes. Deirdre said she'd always dreamt she'd witness some phenomenon or other, and kept a loaded camera handy. That night on the rippled strand the moment she had been waiting for arrived at last, but of course she hadn't brought along her camera.

Episode 3 of our story shows us the PAST PERFECT TENSE, SIMPLE and CONTINUOUS aspects. When we are relating a past event and we want to indicate that something else happened prior to the time of that main event we use the past perfect tense for this. The terms *past perfect* and *pluperfect* are synonymous but the former is preferred in English grammars. The past perfect can be seen as the past of the simple past, or the past of the present perfect.

By the way, on a matter of punctuation did you notice in *she'd always dreamt she'd witness ...* above, that the contraction *she'd* can have two different expansions - *she had* and *she would.* Something similar also occurs with *she's,* etc. Contracted forms (short forms) are acceptable even in written English now.

The time line below uses arrows to indicate back reference from the past to the past perfect.

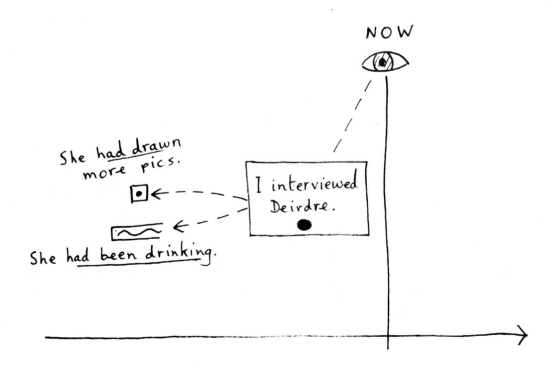

Figure 3. Time line for past perfect (simple and continuous) and past simple.

Now we will put the present perfect and the past perfect tenses together in our list form. As a mnemonic, remember present perfect = *have/has* while past perfect = *had*, plus the main verb (in the form of the past participle) of course.

TENSE	EXAMPLE	USE
PRESENT PERFECT S.	*She has entered a competition.*	recent event or life experience
PRESENT PERFECT C.	*She has been drawing.*	continuous up to now
PAST PERFECT S.	*She had drawn more pictures.*	event or life experience before main past reference
PAST PERFECT C.	*She had been drinking.*	concurrent event before main past reference

Table 3. Present perfect and past perfect tenses.

2.8 FUTURE PERFECT

TENSE SITUATIONS - EPISODE IV (final episode)

> I hope Deirdre wins the art competition; she has certainly put a lot of effort into it. By the end of next week she **will have drawn** (FUTURE PERFECT SIMPLE) 100 still lifes, from which she will choose the best 50. Timewise, she **will have been working** (FUTURE PERFECT CONTINUOUS) steadily at her shell-pink desk for seven solid weeks. I don't think Deirdre will want to see bananas or grapes for some time.

Episode 4 of our story exemplifies the FUTURE PERFECT TENSE, which is the last in a neat list which will need just a little expansion later.

We use the future perfect to look back on a recent event or life experience from a future point in time (compare with the present perfect). The future perfect may also be used to express the likelihood of the completion of an event (at a distance) before now (*by* = at or before), e.g. *They will have touched down by now.*

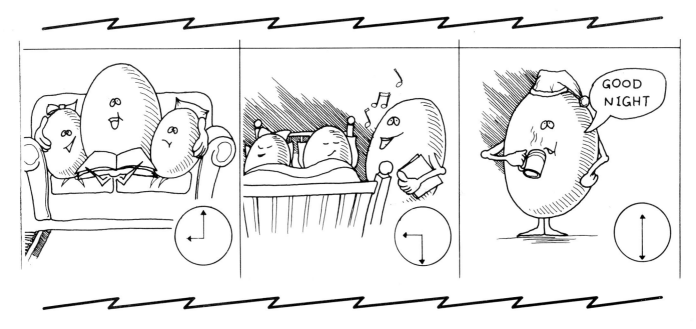

From *Teaching Tenses* by R. Aitken (Longman). Irregular verbs - present or past simple.

Time now to include all the perfect tenses on our list:

TENSE	EXAMPLE	USE
PRESENT SIMPLE	*She draws pictures.*	regular/habitual
PRESENT CONTINUOUS	*She is drawing pictures.*	happening now
PAST SIMPLE	*She drew an alien.*	past event (non-concurrent)
PAST CONTINUOUS	*She was drawing wine.*	concurrent past event
FUTURE SIMPLE	*She will draw blood.*	prediction (non-concurrent event)
FUTURE CONTINUOUS	*She will be drawing the pension.*	prediction of concurrent event
PRESENT PERFECT S.	*She has entered a competition.*	recent event or life experience
PRESENT PERFECT C.	*She has been drawing.*	continuous up to now
PAST PERFECT S.	*She had drawn more pictures.*	event or life experience before main past reference
PAST PERFECT C.	*She had been drinking.*	concurrent event before main past reference
FUTURE PERFECT S.	*She will have drawn 100.*	predicted to have happened by a future time
FUTURE PERFECT C.	*She will have been drawing for 7 weeks.*	continuous event up to a future time (duration stated)

Table 4. Tenses including all perfect aspects.

From *Advanced Communication Games* by J. Hadfield (Longman). Practising the past continuous.

2.9 REVIEW ALL TENSES

And now we shall read the abridged version of the whole story, with the past perfect in a more comfortable position, for revision purposes. Try to match a mental picture with each tense.

Deirdre Charcoal **draws (PRESENT SIMPLE)** quite a lot, indoors and out.
I'm sure she **is drawing (PRESENT CONTINUOUS)** now, under the window.

In 1996 she **drew (PAST SIMPLE)** an alien on Sandymount Strand.
When I knocked on the door she **was drawing (PAST CONTINUOUS)** wine.

She **had drawn (PAST PERFECT SIMPLE)** extra pictures for *The Echo* that morning.
But she **had been drinking (PAST PERFECT CONTINUOUS)** between the strokes.

She **will draw (FUTURE SIMPLE)** blood when she hears about the book.
She **will be drawing (FUTURE CONTINUOUS)** the pension by the time it's published.

Deirdre **has entered (PRESENT PERFECT SIMPLE)** an art competition.
She **has been working (PRESENT PERFECT CONTINUOUS)** hard for 6 weeks.

By next week she **will have drawn (FUTURE PERFECT SIMPLE)** 100 pictures.
She **will have been working (FUTURE PERFECT CONTINUOUS)** steadily for 7 weeks.

T2.4   Fill in the tenses in the right hand column below.

EXAMPLE	TENSE
1. *What will your Ma say?*	
2. *She'd waited as long as possible.*	
3. *Have you been clubbing in the caves?*	
4. *They'll have taken everything by then.*	
5. *I did everything I could.*	
6. *They'd been preparing to leave.*	
7. *I was looking to see if she was looking.*	
8. *Delaney's gone back on the hard stuff.*	
9. *How's it going?*	
10. *How long will they have been driving?*	

2.10 FUTURE TIME - *WILL* AND *GOING TO*

I have been implying above that the future tense in English is represented by *will*. English in fact doesn't have a future tense in the strict sense of inflecting the verb itself. To refer to future time we have two popular choices: 1) the auxiliary verb *will* followed by the bare infinitive; 2) *be going to* followed by the infinitive. Other choices are dealt with in 2.11.

Will, besides predictions, is used for promises and instant decisions. *Going to* is used for plans, intentions, imminent happenings.

Observe the following sentence (in normal speech *will* is contracted to *'ll* unless emphasis is required):
  I'm going to see Les Miserables, *I'll see you when I get back.*

Notice that if the two forms are transposed a curious semantic change occurs:
  I'll see Les Miserables, *I'm going to see you when I get back.*

The frequency of use of the *going to* form obliges TEFL grammars to include it as a future tense. Before looking at the complete list (table 6), perhaps you would like to try task 2.5 on the next page.

4 Work in pairs. Complete one of these dialogues and practise it.

A: I'm going to be a racing driver.
B: dangerous
A: isn't | all right
B: crash | get killed
A: won't
B: find a job
A: will | good driver
B: sure | all right
A: course

A: I'm going to be a doctor.
B: have to study | seven years
A: know | I don't mind
B: finish your studies
A: will
B: have | really hard life
A: interesting
B: have to work very long hours
A: know | don't mind
B: OK − if that's what you want.
A: is

1 🔘 Read the dialogue and then practise it in pairs.

A: I'm going to hitchhike round the world.
B: Oh, that's very dangerous.
A: No, it isn't. I'll be all right.
B: Where will you sleep?
A: Oh, I don't know. In youth hostels. Cheap hotels.
B: You'll get lost.
A: No, I won't.
B: You won't get lifts.
A: Yes, I will.
B: What will you do for money?
A: I'll take money with me.
B: You haven't got enough.
A: If I need money I'll find jobs.
B: Well . . . are you sure you'll be all right?
A: Of course I'll be all right.

5 Make up and practise a short conversation beginning:

    A: 'I'm going to get married.'
or A: 'I'm going to work in a circus.'
or A: 'I'm going to be a teacher.'
or A: 'I'm going to ski down Everest.'
or A: 'I'm going to be a pilot.'

From *New Cambridge English 1* by Swan & Walter (CUP). Future with *will* for predictions (with a *going to* introduction in the dialogues).

Correctly reorder the information in the table below. Ideally, the list should be photocopied and the sections cut out and mounted; then the task is performed as pair or small group work. This ensures more enjoyment, which usually ensures more learning (keep this in mind when your students are to do a matching activity). The first column should be ordered as given.

TENSE	EXAMPLE	USE
1. PRESENT SIMPLE	a) It'll be alright on the night.	i) prediction of concurrent event
2. PRESENT CONTINUOUS	b) We'd been trying to get it started.	ii) predicted to have happened by a future time
3. PAST SIMPLE	c) The plant had grown a foot in our absence.	iii) continuous event up to a future time - duration stated
4. PAST CONTINUOUS	d) They'll have been talking for ten hours come midnight.	iv) plan/intention
5. FUTURE WITH *GOING TO*	e) Sister Stan made her point.	v) regular, habitual
6. FUTURE SIMPLE/ FUTURE WITH *WILL*	f) I was just looking at it.	vi) prediction (non-concurrent event)
7. FUTURE CONTINUOUS	g) You just never listen, do you?	vii) concurrent event before main past reference
8. PRESENT PERFECT S.	h) Bill will be seeing his secretary Monday.	viii) recent event or life experience
9. PRESENT PERFECT C.	i) How long have you been telling that joke?	ix) happening now
10. PAST PERFECT S.	j) That's torn it.	x) event or life experience before main past reference
11. PAST PERFECT C.	k) She's putting up a good fight.	xi) concurrent past event
12. FUTURE PERFECT S.	l) They'll have destroyed half the rainforests by 2015.	xii) continuous up to now
13. FUTURE PERFECT C.	m) You're not going to watch Casablanca *again, are you?*	xiii) past event (non-concurrent)

Table 5. All tenses - single examples (task).

TENSE	EXAMPLE	USE
PRESENT SIMPLE	*She draws pictures.*	regular/habitual
PRESENT CONTINUOUS	*She is drawing pictures.*	happening now
PAST SIMPLE	*She drew an alien.*	past event (non-concurrent)
PAST CONTINUOUS	*She was drawing wine.*	concurrent past event
FUTURE WITH *GOING TO*	*I'm going to pose for Deirdre.*	plan/intention
FUTURE SIMPLE/ FUTURE WITH *WILL*	*She will draw blood.*	prediction (non-concurrent event)
FUTURE CONTINUOUS	*She will be drawing the pension.*	prediction of concurrent event
PRESENT PERFECT S.	*She has entered a competition.*	recent event or life experience
PRESENT PERFECT C.	*She has been drawing.*	continuous up to now
PAST PERFECT S.	*She had drawn more pictures.*	event or life experience before main past reference
PAST PERFECT C.	*She had been drinking.*	concurrent event before main past reference
FUTURE PERFECT S.	*She will have drawn 100.*	predicted to have happened by a future time
FUTURE PERFECT C.	*She will have been drawing for 7 weeks.*	continuous event up to a future time (duration stated)

Table 6. All tenses, grouped.

The treatment of *going to,* as with other forms in the tables above, is brief. We could have included an example of a future continuous with *going to,* such as *we're going to be canning strawberries for six weeks,* or a past intention, e.g. *we were going to tell you,* but these may be taken for granted.

2.11 OTHER FUTURES

[T2.6] Become aware of two different time references for the present continuous and observe three other futures by joining the examples with their uses in the table below.

EXAMPLE	USE
1. So we're playing in Old Trafford?	a) happening at time of speaking
2. Oh no! She's eating the worm!	b) plan - already decided
3. We'll play, we'll play, don't worry.	c) arrangement ('diary' future)
4. Our train leaves at nine.	d) timetable
5. We're gonna play our hearts out.	e) promise

Table 7. Present and futures (task).

2.12 *USED TO* AND *WOULD*

> Deirdre **used to** live (past state) on a dairy farm in Dorset.
> Every morning she **would** rise (past habitual event) at dawn to do the milking.

Used to and *would* are not tenses but are treated somewhat similarly in many coursebooks, so they could be shaped into our list as below. (*Used to* and *would* are auxiliary verbs - see 12.2)

There is a choice of forms for *used to* in the negative and interrogative, although as these are little used there's not much need to teach them:

> *She didn't use(d) to; she usedn't to; she usen't to; she used not to.*
> *Did she use(d) to? Used she to?*   (*Did* + *used to* is becoming unacceptable.)

T2.7 Complete the table below by writing *habitual event in the past* and *state in the past* in the appropriate blank sections a) and b).

'TENSE'	EXAMPLE	USE
USED TO	*She used to own a Land Rover.* *She used to think nettles were useless.*	a)
USED TO/WOULD	*She used to/would rise at dawn.* *She used to/would go for a walk in the evening.*	b)

Table 8. *Used to* and *would* (task).

2.13 STATIVE AND DYNAMIC VERBS

When a verb has a **stative** sense, i.e. when it describes a state, emotion, sensation, then it usually cannot occur in a continuous tense. Verbs that cannot be or are not being used in a stative sense are called **dynamic verbs.** Common stative verbs are *seem, know, understand, own, want, see, smell, prefer.* The rule is flexible to a degree, e.g. a certain continuity is carried by *Are you understanding me okay?*

The examples below show that [1] the verb *like* is always stative, but *think* can be used [2b] statively or [2c] dynamically. The grammar in [2a] and [2c] is also different.

> [1]   **I am liking you.*
> [2a] **I am thinking you are nice.*
> [2b] *I think you are nice.*
> [2c] *I am thinking about it.*

2.14 CONTINUOUS ACT VERBS

Verbs such as *live, work, rain, stay, wait, sleep, be,* and especially in intransitive use *sing, dance, study, teach,* may be called **continuous act verbs** because they give no indication of their duration/termination. In ELT this property becomes most noticeable when the difference between the present perfect simple and continuous is almost neutralised by the aspect of continuity within the verb itself. Observe:

> [3] *We have lived here for 30 years.*
> [4] *We have been living here for 30 years.*

T2.8 A student at advanced level asks you to explain the difference in meaning, if any, between [3] and [4] above. How do you reply?

3 The Present Perfect

Many TEFL course participants experience difficulty in coming to terms with the present perfect. For this reason I have devoted an extra chapter to a quick revision of same and a short discussion on some interesting aspects of the perfect aspect present tense.

3.1 PRESENT PERFECT REVISITED

T3.1 Two of the example sentences below are misplaced. Match them properly.

EXAMPLE	USE
1. *Have you done your homework yet?* -- 2. *Has she (ever) been to Peru?*	a) recent event with focus on the present
3. *She has entered a competition.* -- 4. *I've directed 3 movies.*	b) life experience/achievement, focus on the present

Table 9. Present perfect simple - two main uses (task).

3.2 PAST SIMPLE OR PRESENT PERFECT?

In AmE and some other dialects, notably IrE, the past simple is often used instead of the present perfect. *Did you do your homework yet?* would sound odd to British ears, where *Have you done ...* would be more acceptable. American and Irish speakers of English would find nothing wrong with either sentence. However, *Did she go to Peru?* (life experience use) would be rare for present perfect interpretation without the word *ever* inserted. Thus *Did she ever/Did you ever...?* is quite common outside of Britain.

In assessing English as an international language, then, one should not penalize the student for producing the past simple in lieu of the present perfect when a time adverbial like *yet* or *ever* or some other suitable context marker is included.

On another dialectal note, the colloquial and mainly southern IrE 'after' in e.g. *He's after breaking the vase* is used unwittingly by some Irish teachers in their classroom language. Students find it curious but don't seem to pick it up and of course are not asked to learn it.

EXAMPLE	USE
He didn't catch anything yet. *You dropped your purse, Ma'am.* *Did you ever ... ?*	AmE/IrE variety of present perfect
You're after dropping your purse.	IrE variety of present perfect (recent event)

Table 10. AmE and IrE varieties of present perfect.

4 Nouns

In this chapter we will look at three categories of noun:

      1) Countable/uncountable   **2) Collective**   **3) Irregular**

4.1 COUNTABLE AND UNCOUNTABLE NOUNS

4.1.1 Definition

What is the difference (grammatical) between *apple* and *serenity*? You can say *an apple/some apples* but you can't say **a serenity/some serenities*. We use the terms **count(able)** and **uncount(able)** for these two major classes of noun. As a broad definition, count nouns can be counted, and used in the singular or plural. Uncount nouns cannot be counted and take only singular verbs. Observe the table below.

COUNT NOUNS	UNCOUNT NOUNS
cake	cake
yoghurt	yoghurt
sheep	sand
abacus	wool
king	- - - - - - - - - - - -
child	honesty
month	physics
suggestion	chess

Uncount nouns may be divided into **mass nouns** (above the dotted line) and **abstract nouns** (below the dotted line), although many grammars call all uncount nouns *mass nouns*.

4.1.2 Alternative countable and uncountable forms

a) units vs. mass
      some/four cakes, cabbages, lambs : some cake, cabbage, lamb

b) measures, etc.
      Three teas/sugars/yoghurts simply means *three cups of tea, lumps of sugar, tubs of yoghurt*, etc.

c) classifications
      the wines of Province; a low-fat cheese, etc.

d) artistic/literary product vs. activity
      some/four works of Goya : do some work

4.2 COLLECTIVE NOUNS

Collective nouns refer to groups and so are also called **group nouns**. They can take a singular or plural verb, accordingly as the members of the group are seen as united or separate (please note that animal groupings such as *herd, pride, gaggle, etc,* do not automatically fall under this category in TEFL):

      The government is intact.
      The government are of different minds on the issue.

American formal English, however, prefers the singular verb. Other collective nouns include *army, audience, family, flock, group, jury, staff, team, company.*

4.2 IRREGULAR FORMS

Nouns which usually cause problems are

1) **Summation plurals,** e.g. *trousers, scissors,* etc. These often get treated as singular in certain (English-speaking) dialect areas, e.g. *Have you got a scissors? The scissors is over there,* etc. Technically, however, one is expected to use (and teach) *are* and *a pair of ... is* with these.
2) **Uncountable nouns ending in 's'** e.g. *news, measles, linguistics, darts* (game) etc, which may take a little getting used to.
3) **Nouns having the same singular and plural form,** e.g. *sheep, deer, salmon, series,* etc.
4) **-f to -ves,** e.g. *knife-knives, shelf-shelves,* but *roof-roofs,* and *hoof-hoofs/hooves,* etc.

Grammar in use

1 Look at the text.

a Answer the questions.
1 What is it about?
2 What is the purpose of the diet?
3 Who is it for?
4 Why is it called the Pyramid diet?

b Read the text and complete the diagram.

2 Discuss these questions.
1 Is the Pyramid diet sensible?
2 Is it appropriate for everyone?
3 Would it provide an interesting diet?

Rules

1 Look at the two groups of words.

a Answer the questions.
1 Which can we make plural?
2 Which can we use *a* or *an* with?

_____ *nouns*	_____ *nouns*
potato apple vitamin	bread pasta calcium

b Write the words *uncountable* and *countable* at the top of the correct columns.

c Find more examples of both types of noun in the text.

➤ Check the rules for countable and uncountable nouns in **Grammar Reference 8.1**.

THE PYRAMID

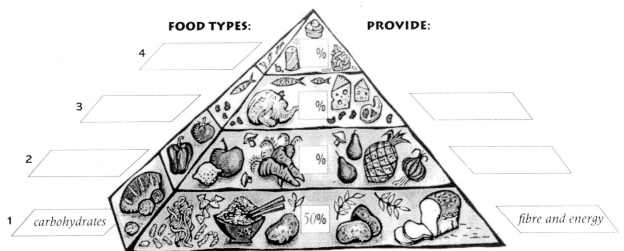

FOOD TYPES: **PROVIDE:**

4
3
2
1 *carbohydrates*   *fibre and energy*

50%

We've had them all – the High Fibre diet, the Protein diet, the Hip and Thigh diet. And here's the latest – the Pyramid diet. But this isn't a diet to help people lose weight. It's a diet for a healthy life. The Pyramid diet is very simple. Different kinds of food are at different levels of the pyramid. The higher up the pyramid, the less you should eat. At the bottom of the pyramid are complex carbohydrates like bread, pasta and potatoes. These provide fibre and energy. About 50% of your diet should be complex carbohydrates. At the second level are fruit and vegetables, such as apples and carrots. These should be about 30% of your diet. They provide vitamins and minerals as well as fibre. Above fruit and vegetables are the protein-rich foods like meat, fish, beans and cheese. These also provide a lot of calcium. These protein-rich foods should be about 18% of your diet. At the top of the pyramid are fat oil and sugar. We should eat as little as possible of things at this level.

From *Lifelines Pre-intermediate* by T. Hutchinson (OUP). Countable and uncountable nouns.

5 Quantifiers

5.1 Definition

Quantifiers come under the heading of *determiners*. Determiners are words in the noun phrase that can come before an adjective (and noun). These also include the articles *the* and *a,* and the demonstratives *this, that,* etc. Quantifiers, or quantitative/quantitive adjectives, are a closed set of words like *all, both, half, some, any, another, enough, either, more, several, a lot, few*, etc, and the numerals.

5.2 *How many?* and *How much?*

EFL coursebooks usually teach *How many...?* and *How much...?* accompanied by some corresponding count and uncount nouns at elementary level, e.g.

> *How many eggs are there in the fridge? How much milk is there in the trolly?*

5.3 *Many* and *much* (and *lots of/a lot of*)

In the affirmative, *many,* and especially *much,* tend to be formal (notice the incongruity of *There were many fans at that gig, man*). In informal English *lots of/a lot of* is preferred, and it's advisable to teach these early because they can be used with both count and uncount nouns, e.g.

> *There are lots of/a lot of pennies falling out there.*
> *There's lots of/a lot of rain falling out there.*

There's + plural, e.g. *There's lots of/a lot of pennies,* is generally acceptable in informal spoken English.

5.4 *A few* and *a little*

A few (aspirins) and a *little* (Vaseline) would also be introduced in coursebooks with count and uncount nouns, e.g.

> *A few beers, a little music.*

Not until intermediate level, however, would *few* (social workers) and *little* (funding) be on the syllabus, as the connotation of scarcity here has to be understood despite the almost identical form with *a few* and *a little*. Students should check these words in their bilingual dictionaries and be aware of the corresponding forms in their language(s).

5.5 *Some* and *any* with plural and uncountable nouns

To explain the uses of *some* and *any* at elementary level we can make do with the rule which says that *some* is used in affirmative sentences, and *any* is used in questions and negatives:

> *Tom's got <u>some</u> aardvarks.*
> *Have you got <u>any</u> tickets?*
> *We haven't got <u>any</u> sugar, but we do need <u>some</u>.*

There are some difficulties, however. The first one is explaining *any* in an affirmative sentence, such as:

> *There's rarely <u>any</u> trouble.*

This is explained by pointing out that *rarely* (like *hardly, seldom,* etc.) is a negative adverb.

For exceptions such as

> *Have you got <u>some</u> money?*

ELT grammars usually state that a positive answer is expected. While this may not be fully explanatory it has proved satisfactory when simplicity is required.

Language focus

'Some' and 'any'; object pronouns; expressing likes and dislikes

1 Can you cook?

Discussion

Do you like cooking? Do you know any recipes? Tell the class.

2 What are they making?

Listening
Extra practice • WB Ex. 1

🔲 Look at the recipes and listen.

Pat and Anne want to make something. What is it?
Can they make it? What *can* they make?

PANCAKES

You need:
2 cups of flour
1 cup of milk
1 cup of water
1 egg

SHORTBREAD BISCUITS

You need:
350g of flour
225g of butter
100g of sugar
some salt

3 What have we got?

'some' and 'any'
Extra practice •
WB Exs. 2, 4
Extra practice •
TB Ws. 15.1

3.1 What do you say?

How do you say these sentences in your language?

We've got some eggs.
We haven't got any butter.
Have you got any sugar?

What do 'some' and 'any' mean in your language?

3.2 A grammar puzzle

When do you say 'some'? When do you say 'any'?

Look at the sentences below.
With your neighbour, work out a rule.

You say 'some' when...   You say 'any' when...

We need some butter.
For breakfast, I have some bread and milk.
We've got some eggs.

From *Cambridge English for Schools; Student's Book One* by Littlejohn & Hicks (CUP). *Some* and *any*.

6 Pronouns

We have dealt with personal pronouns in chapter 1. Five further types are introduced here.

6.1 POSSESSIVE DETERMINER PRONOUNS

	singular	plural
1st person	*my*	*our*
2nd person	*your*	*your*
3rd person	*her/his/its*	*their*

These are also called *possessive adjectives*.
Be careful with the spelling of *its*. The apostrophe indicates the shortened form of *it is*, not possessive:
   It's *the dog that bit* **its** *tail.*
Nouns with *'s*, e.g. *John's; Hong Kong's,* are said to be in the **genitive** or **possessive** case.

6.2 POSSESSIVE INDEPENDENT PRONOUNS

	singular	plural
1st person	*mine*	*ours*
2nd person	*yours*	*yours*
3rd person	*hers/his*	*theirs*

Students may require some time to acquire *a friend of mine*, etc, usually going through some normal error stages in the process. Just use gentle correction and TLC for painless progress.

6.3 REFLEXIVE PRONOUNS

	singular	plural
1st person	*myself*	*ourselves*
2nd person	*yourself*	*yourselves*
3rd person	*herself/himself/itself*	*themselves*

We use reflexive pronouns [1] when subject and object are the same person, [2] for emphasis, and [3] to mean *unaccompanied:*
   [1] *Mary hurt* **herself***.*
   [2] *The house* **itself** *wasn't too bad.*
   [3] *She'll have to do it (by)* **herself***.*

6.4 DEMONSTRATIVE PRONOUNS

This, that, these and *those* are adjectives before a noun and pronouns on their own. They can be seen as 'pointers', referring to [1] physical things, or [2] part of the discourse:
   [1] *Is* **this** *yours? One of* **these** *gets me any of* **those***.*
   [2] *But* **this** *is only half the problem.* **That's** *not what I meant.*

6.5 INDEFINITE PRONOUNS

Anyone, everybody, everything, no one/no-one, nobody, someone, anything, nothing, etc.
Indefinite personal pronouns are singular, but may take a plural, 'sex-neutral' pronoun, e.g.
> ***Anyone/no one*** can set ***themselves*** up as a clairvoyant.
> ***Someone*** is/***everyone*** is throwing ***their*** money away on the nag.

7 Adjectives

7.1 TYPES OF ADJECTIVE - FUNCTIONAL

T7.1 In the table below 1) match the type of adjective with the examples/set, leaving the middle column intact; 2) write the words OPEN and CLOSED in the correct sections a) and b).

TYPE OF SET	TYPE OF ADJ	EXAMPLES/SET
a)_____	1. qualitative	(i) *this, that, these* and *those.*
	2. classifying	(ii) *all, any, another, each, little/a little* ... (total approximately 20, not counting numerals or *of*+ types).
b)_____	3. demonstrative	(iii) *electric, Korean, medical, legal, oak, pregnant* ...
	4. quantitative	(iv) *dark, efficient, friendly, fast, hard, funny, soft* ...

Table 11. Functional types of adjective (task).

7.2 TYPES OF ADJECTIVE - GRAMMATICAL

7.2.1 *-ing* participial adjectives
-ing participial adjectives are derived from verbs, e.g.
> *amusing, interesting, demeaning, humiliating, tempting.*

Adjectives ending in *-ing* which are derived from nouns, e.g *enterprising, neighbouring,* are not called *-ing* participials. (Note this hair-splitting is not for the EFL classroom; however, a familiarity with the terminology is required for more relevant topics later, and for professional confidence.)

7.2.2 Past participial adjectives
Many past participles can serve as adjectives, e.g.
> *amused, interested, fallen, embarrassed, forsaken, exhausted, elated*

Some words may look like past participles but they are adjectives only, having no corresponding verb, e.g. *downtrodden (*to downtread ...),* or being only partly related to a verb, e.g. *drunken.*

N.B. A common error is confusion between e.g. *interesting* and *interested,* etc. To explain the difference you may point out that the former is causal whereas the latter describes the person's state. How far this helps the learning is an open question, of course. Add communicative practice to ensure results.

7.2.3 Attributive and predicative adjectives

These criteria pertain to the position of the adjective: [1] attributive is before the noun; [2] predicative is not before a noun and usually in the predicate. There may be some semantic change, even restrictions:

[1] *the great famine : my elder sister : * the ablaze house*
[2] *?the famine was great : *my sister is elder : the house is ablaze*

7.3 ORDER OF ADJECTIVES

When a number of qualitative and/or classifying adjectives occur before a noun, they usually follow a certain order. Below is a (rather overloaded) noun phrase with various sub-types of adjective.

1) Sort out the noun phrase by matching each adjective with its type and putting these into an acceptable order.
2) Indicate which types would go under the macro types *qualitative* and *classifying*.

	COLOUR	MATERIAL	NATIONALITY	SIZE	PURPOSE	QUALITY	
A	Victorian	old	ceramic	water	red	big	jug

Of course, the ordering rule can be broken somewhat for emphasis, etc.

7.4 NON-GRADABLE OR 'LIMIT' ADJECTIVES

Adjectives at the end of a scale, such as *boiling - freezing, huge - tiny, brilliant - terrible, fascinating, terrifying, flabbergasted,* etc, cannot be pre-modified with intensifiers (see 8.3.5) such as *very, fairly,* etc, but interestingly can be with emphasizers such as *absolutely, really,* etc.

A 'Scale' and 'limit' adjectives

(absolutely) terrible	(very) bad	OK	(very) good	(absolutely) marvellous
awful				wonderful
dreadful				great
				terrific

30.3 Complete these dialogues using the correct limit adjective in the correct form (-*ing* or -*ed*).

  1 A: Was it very tiring?
    B: Yes we were absolutely ....
  2 A: I was very interested in her talk.
    B: Yes it was absolutely ....
  3 A: Maria said it was a frightening film.
    B: Yes it was absolutely ....
  4 A: It was a surprising decision, wasn't it?
    B: Yes I was absolutely ....
  5 A: Was it very cold?
    B: Oh yes, it was ....

30.4 Can you think of an adjective from the opposite page to describe how the people felt in each of these situations?

  1 They walked about ten miles in the morning, then spent the afternoon helping some friends to cut down some trees.
  2 From the description in the travel brochure, they expected a beautiful big villa by the sea. In actual fact it was quite small, not very nice, and miles from the beach.

From *English Vocabulary in Use - Pre-intermediate & Intermediate* by S. Redman (CUP). 'Scale' and 'limit' adjectives including *-ing* participial and past participial (*-ed*) adjectives.

8 Adverbs

8.1 TERMINOLOGY AND FUNCTIONS

An **adverb** is a word giving us information about how, where, when or to what degree something is done, e.g. *do it quickly*, *go out/home*, *leave today*, *completely destroyed*. An **adverbial** is an adverb or any other group of words, not necessarily containing an adverb, which functions as an adverb, e.g. *as fast as possible, under the clock, after 8, unfortunately*.

English adverbs do a lot of work. An adverb can modify a verb, an adjective, an adverb, even a whole sentence (see 21.1). Following are some types. Please note that *adverb = adverbial* where applicable.

8.2 TYPES OF ADVERB

T8.1 Match the types of adverb with the examples.

TYPE OF ADVERB	EXAMPLE
1. Manner	a) *yesterday, at two o'clock, over the summer, soon*
2. Time	b) *always, often, sometimes, seldom, never*
3. Place and direction	c) *slowly, quickly, fast, hard, peacefully, coolly*
4. Frequency	d) *extensively, partially, completely, totally*
5. Degree	e) *underneath, northward, below, abroad, home*

8.3 POSITION OF ADVERBS

8.3.1 Adverbs of manner
These have a great deal of flexibility, e.g.
> *(Hurriedly,)° she (hurriedly)° dressed (hurriedly)°.*

8.3.2 Adverbs of definite time and adverbs of place
These usually go in end position, but may be fronted for topicality or emphasis, e.g.
> *(Tomorrow)° they're coming here (tomorrow)°.*
> *(In Xian)° there are thousands of terracotta soldiers (in Xian)°.*

With respect to order, place usually precedes time, especially when the adverb of place is one of the closed set type (*here, there*, etc.), e.g.
> *I'll see you <u>there</u> <u>at nine</u>.*

8.3.3 Adverbs of (general) frequency
These go after the auxiliary verb, e.g.
> *I have <u>often</u> walked down this street before.*

If there is no aux., the adverb goes immediately before the main verb, or after the linking verb *to be*, e.g.
> *She <u>rarely</u> smiles.*   *He is <u>seldom</u> right.*

These rules of position may be bent somewhat for emphasis, and *sometimes* and some other frequency adverbs can go at the start or end of a sentence.

8.3.4 Adverbs of degree

These tend to go before the verb, but many may also fit in end position, e.g.

> He (completely)° exonerated them (completely)°.

Many adverbs of degree (and adverbs of manner) modify adjectives or past participles, e.g.

> *partially* deaf   *completely* exonerated.

8.3.5 Intensifiers

Intensifiers are not included in the table above. They comprise *very, quite, pretty, fairly,* etc, and their main function is to premodify adjectives and adverbs. *Very* and *pretty* can premodify the degree adverb *much*.

always	never	occasionally	every day
hardly ever	once/twice a week/month		
most mornings	every couple of weeks		

2   Work in pairs. Use the picture cues below (and your own ideas) to ask and answer as in the examples.

A: *Do you have a bath in the morning?*
B: *No, hardly ever. (I hardly ever have a bath in the morning.)*
A: *How often do you travel to work by bus?*
B: *Once a week. (I travel to work by bus once a week.)*

STUDENT A
Find out about Student B's morning routine. Use the weak form of *do* where appropriate and try to make your questions sound polite. Use the pictures to help you and ask any other questions you want to ask.

STUDENT B
Reply to Student A's questions. Give information about your morning routine, using expressions from the box in Exercise 1.

3   In groups, report back on any interesting things which you have found out about your partner's morning routine. Example:
'*Anna and I both get up at the same time, but she eats a cooked breakfast . . .*'

From *Intermediate Matters* by J.Bell & R. Gower (Longman). Frequency adverbs and phrases.

9 Degrees of Comparison

9.1 COMPARISON OF ADJECTIVES

POSITIVE	COMPARATIVE	SUPERLATIVE
1. hard happy	harder happier	(the) hardest (the) happiest
2. clever	cleverer/more clever	(the) cleverest/most clever
3. tragic flirtatious	more tragic more flirtatious	(the) most tragic (the) most flirtatious
4. good bad	better worse	(the) best (the) worst

Adjectives can be economically divided into 4 types for comparative and superlative formation, as the above table shows:

1. Monosyllabic, or bisyllabic ending in -*y*: -*er*, -*est*.
2. Bisyllabic usually with short vowels and final 'soft' consonant (or other phonological properties whic lend to ease of suffixation with -*er* and -*est*): free choice of -*er*, -*est* or *more, most*.
3. Other bisyllabic, or polysyllabic: *more, most*.
4. Irregular.

9.2 COMPARISON OF ADVERBS

POSITIVE	COMPARATIVE	SUPERLATIVE
1. hard fast	harder faster	hardest fastest
2. quickly/quick slowly/slow	more quickly/quicker more slowly/slower	most quickly/quickest most slowly/slowest
3. sensibly seldom	more sensibly more seldom	most sensibly most seldom
4. well badly	better worse	best worst

Adverbs can be divided into 4 types for forming the comparative and superlative, as the above table shows:

1. Adverbs identical in form to adjectives:
   comparative and superlative formed as adjectives: -*er*, -*est*.
2. -*ly* adverbs with alternative adjectival form for informal and restricted uses:
   choice of *more, most* + -*ly*, or adjectival -*er*, -*est*.
3. Polysyllabic including -*ly*, or bisyllabic without -*ly*: *more, most*.
4. Irregular.

Grammar and practice

1 Comparisons

The reading text includes a number of comparison phrases. Without looking back at the text, try to fill the gaps in these extracts. The first one has been done for you.

1 When it comes to *less* important things, like deciding where to go on holiday, it's a different matter.
2 The battle of wills is _____ more serious _____ simply deciding between a soap opera and a sports programme.
3 Some people are naturally _____ dominant _____ others.
4 The _____ dominant person in the family tries to lead.
5 Men generally have a g_____ need to appear to be in physical control.
6 Women are not _____ interested in physical control _____ in emotional control.
7 Most kids are far _____ innocent, far _____ knowing than their parents realize.

Now look back at the text and check your answers.

2 Comparative and superlative adjectives

A What are the comparative and superlative forms of these adjectives?

bad   common*   far   friendly*   good
high*   important*   old   strange*   thin*

* Think of two or three more adjectives which have comparative and superlative forms like these.

B Here are some phrases which are used with comparative adjectives.

a bit   far   a little   a lot   much   slightly

Which phrases are used to compare two things which are very different from each other, and which are used to compare things which are almost the same?

C Before continuing, check your understanding of comparative and superlative adjectives in the Grammar reference on pages 202–203.

3 Practice

A Compare these pairs of famous partners using as many different expressions of comparison as possible.

Examples *Tom is heavier than Jerry. Tom is (just) as clever as Jerry. Tom is less loveable than Jerry.*

B Write sentences comparing these three photographs of people at work.

1 First, compare pairs of jobs, e.g. the disc jockey and the priest.
2 Now compare all three people's lives, using superlative expressions.

Examples *I think the fisherman has **the hardest life.** The disc jockey is probably **the richest of the three.***

From *New First Certificate Masterclass* by Haines & Stewart (OUP). Comparative and superlative adjectives.

10 The Passive Voice

10.1 DEFINITION

Observe the following sentences:

      [1] *Deirdre drew an alien.*
      [2] *An alien was drawn by Deirdre.*

In [1] the first thing (person) mentioned is doing the action. This sentence is said to be in the **active voice**. In [2] the first thing mentioned is in a passive state, at least as far as the information in the sentence goes. This sentence is said to be in the **passive voice**.

While this is not a very scientific definition, it suits TEFL reasonably well.

10.2 FORM/STRUCTURE

To change a sentence from active to passive: a) move the logical object (in [1] above this is *an alien*) to the position of grammatical subject (the beginning of the sentence), b) insert the verb *be* as an auxiliary verb in the tense required (*was*), c) follow with the **past participle** of the main verb (*drawn*), which must be a transitive verb of course, and optionally, d) end with *by* and the agent/logical subject (*Deirdre*).

> **the past participle** has two main contexts:
>   1. after the auxiliary *have* in perfect tenses;
>   2. (transitive verbs only) after the verb *be* in passive sentences.

10.3 WHAT DO WE TEACH?

In communicative language teaching we don't, of course, ask our students to carry out such grammatical gymnastics as in 10.2 above. Like much information in this book, this is for the teacher to know, to enable her to increase her professional knowledge and confidence, and to use in the required measure and at the required time. What do we teach? We teach use.

10.4 USES OF THE PASSIVE

There are two major uses of the passive:

1. to focus attention on the object, e.g.
      Fido was hit by a car,
where Fido is our main concern, not the car.

2. to avoid mentioning the agent, e.g.
      The matter is being attended to,
where the person doing the action is not required to be or cannot be mentioned - a favourite with politicians, this one.

Manufacturing processes, and crimes, are popular for practising the present and past passive, e.g.
      The barley is roasted... the hops are added...
      Maurizio Gucci and Gianni Versace were murdered.

10.5 PASSIVE IN TENSES

T10.1 Fill in the right hand column with the passive transformations. The first one has been done for you. You will find that some forms sound strange, indicating that they occur very rarely. Mark these with an 'R'.

TENSE	ACTIVE	PASSIVE
PRESENT SIMPLE	*She draws pictures.*	*Pictures are drawn by her.*
PRESENT CONTINUOUS	*She is drawing fruit.*	
PAST SIMPLE	*She drew an alien.*	
PAST CONTINUOUS	*She was drawing wine.*	
FUTURE SIMPLE	*She'll draw blood.*	
FUTURE WITH *GOING TO*	*She's going to win the competition.*	
FUTURE CONTINUOUS	*She'll be drawing the pension.*	
PRESENT PERFECT S.	*She has drawn U2.*	
PRESENT PERFECT C.	*She has been drawing bananas and grapes.*	
PAST PERFECT S.	*She had drawn more pictures that morning.*	
PAST PERFECT C.	*She had been drinking wine.*	
FUTURE PERFECT S.	*She will have drawn 100 pictures by next Sunday.*	
FUTURE PERFECT C.	*She will have been drawing fruit for 7 weeks.*	

Table 12. Active and passive voice in tenses (task).

SPEAKING AND VOCABULARY

1 Work in pairs. Are these sentences true or false?

Apple makes computers.
Lemons grow on trees.
Gustav Eiffel built the Eiffel Tower.
Marconi invented the radio.
Beethoven composed the Moonlight Sonata.
Leonardo da Vinci painted the Mona Lisa *(La Joconde)*.
Shakespeare wrote Hamlet.
Fleming discovered penicillin.

READING

1 Read *The round-the-world quiz* and choose the correct answer.

The round-the-world quiz

1 Coffee is grown in ...
   a Brazil   b England   c Sweden

2 Daewoo cars are made in ...
   a Switzerland   b Thailand   c Korea

3 Sony computers are made in ...
   a Japan   b the USA   c Germany

From *Reward - Elementary* by S. Greenall (Heinemann). Active and passive, present and past simple.

11 Irregular Verbs

Regular verbs form their past tense and past participle by adding -d or -ed. Verbs which form their past tense and/or past participle in other ways, e.g. with a vowel change, as in *sing, sang, sung*, or even with no change, as in *cut, cut, cut* are irregular. Most grammars and coursebooks have lists of irregular verbs.

T11.1 Below are some verbs set out in the usual three columns. After each verb mark **C** for *correct* or *complete*, or **I** for *incorrect* or *incomplete*, correcting or adding where appropriate. *Incomplete* here means that an alternative form has not been included (AmE = American English).

	INFINITIVE	PAST TENSE	PAST PARTICIPLE	C/I
1	beseech	besought/beseeched	besought/beseeched	—
2	blow	blew	blown/AmE blowed	—
3	dive	dive/AmE dove	dived/AmE dove	—
4	drink	drank	drunk/AmE drank	—
5	dream	dreamt/dreamed	dreamt/dreamed	—
6	forbid	forbade/forbad	forbidden	—
7	hurt	hurt/AmE hurted	hurt	—
8	lie (down)	lay/laid	laid	—
9	mow	mowed	mown	—
10	quit	quit/quitted	quit/quitted	—

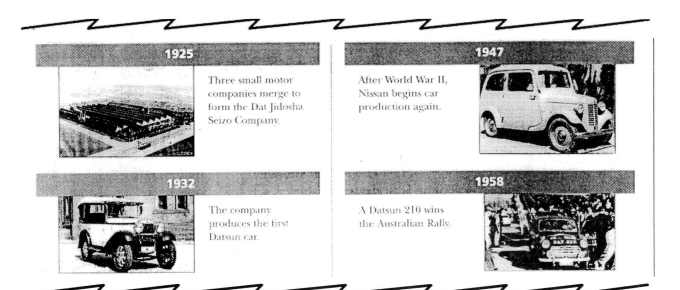

1925 Three small motor companies merge to form the Dat Jidosha Seizo Company.

1947 After World War II, Nissan begins car production again.

1932 The company produces the first Datsun car.

1958 A Datsun 210 wins the Australian Rally.

I Work in pairs. Ask and answer questions about the Nissan Motor Company.

A *What happened in 1925?*
B *Three small motor companies merged.*
A *What happened in 1947?*
B *Nissan began car production again.*

Regular verbs end -ed in the Past Simple tense. Irregular verbs have a special form. There is a table of irregular verbs on page 177.

From *Business Objectives* by V. Hollett (OUP). Past simple, with some basic questions.

40 *A Grammar Course for TEFL Certificate*

12 Modal Auxiliary Verbs

12.1 AUXILIARY VERBS

There are two types of auxiliary verbs: **primary auxiliary verbs**, which comprise *be* (1.5), *have* (2.6.1) and *do* (questions, negatives and emphasis); and the **modal auxiliary verbs**. Modal auxiliary verbs are also called modal auxiliaries, modal verbs or modals. Modal auxiliaries are followed by a main verb (except in cases of inversion, or insertion of one or more primary auxiliaries).

12.2 LIST OF MODALS AND SEMI-MODALS

The following list is of my own construction. *Shall* for future prediction (1st person only) is mainly BrE and rarely now presented in coursebooks. The term *semi-modal* is not used by many TEFL grammars, but serves well to classify some 'left-overs'.

MODALS	*can* *could*	*may* *might*	*will* *would*	*shall* *should*	*ought to* *must*
SEMI-MODALS	*need*	*dare*	*used to*		*have (got) to*

Table 13. Modals and semi-modals.

12.3 DEFINITION OF MODALS

Unlike the primary auxiliaries - *be, have* and *do* - which mainly have a grammatical function, the modal auxiliaries carry meaning. Although it is an overly strong definition of function, you may as a mnemonic interpret *modal* as 'conveying the *mood* or opinion of the speaker', e.g. expressing ability, obligation, advice, possibility, etc.

12.4 USES OF MODALS

Modals are quite versatile in the meanings they convey. For example, *could* has the functions of asking permission, asking for assistance, making requests, expressing ability in the past, expressing possibility, making suggestions. There are also some synonyms, e.g. *can = may = could* in the function of requesting permission, the choice of modal decided mainly by register*.

12.5 STRUCTURE OF MODALS

Modals are not inflected, i.e. there is no *-ed* for past tense, no *-s* for third person singular present and no preceding *do*. The one exception to this is *dare* (see 12.6).

Modals are followed by the bare infinitive (infinitive without *to*), so the modal itself carries the tense, although it is not inflected. *Ought* is usually followed by *to*, then justifying relegation to semi-modal status, but in TEFL *ought to* is treated equally with *should,* etc, as a modal.

*Register is similar in meaning to *style*. Register reflects the relationship between speaker and listener (or writer and reader).

12.6 SEMI-MODALS

Need and *dare* can operate as modals if they are not followed by *to*, and as main verbs if they are, then undergoing any inflexion (tense or 3rd person *-s* marking). *Dare* can undergo some inflexion while remaining a modal. *Need* and *dare* as modals are usually only used in the negative and question form:

> *You needn't finish that tonight. Need you ask?*
> *Dare I ask? I daren't. She didn't dare (to) tell her parents.*

The modal idiom *was able to* (not in table) expresses accomplishment; *could* expresses ability.

12.7 MODAL PERFECT

When a modal is followed by the present perfect, i.e. *have* + past participle, it is usually called the **modal perfect**. The modal perfect is used to express possibility, obligation, assumption, etc, about something in the past. The functions of modals are not necessarily retained when shifted to the perfect aspect, e.g.

> *She might go in there* (possibility). = *She might have gone in there* (possibility).
> *You must tell the president* (obligation). ≠ *You must have told the president* (deduction).

- Hi! Carl? It's Andy. Yeah. How are you? Feeling better?
- Really? Still using a crutch, eh? So you're not back at work yet?
- Two more weeks! That's when the plaster comes off, is it?
- No, I'm fine. The suntan's fading, though. Josie's is, too. She sends love, by the way.
- Yes, yes, I have. I got them back today. They're good. I didn't realize we'd taken so many.
- Yes, the sunset. It's a good one. All of us together on Bob and Marcia's balcony, with the mountains and the snow in the background. It's beautiful. Brings back memories, doesn't it?
- Yes, I know. I'm sorry. At least it was towards the end; it could have been the first day. You only came home two days early.
- Yes, we have. Yesterday, in fact. Bob wrote it and we all signed it. I don't know if it'll do any good, but it's worth a try.
- Yeah. They found it. It arrived on the next flight. Marcia was delighted.
- Sure. Some ups and downs, but generally I think we all got on well and had a great time. Shall we go again next year?

b What happened to Carl?
  – He must have broken his leg. ☐
  – He could have broken his arm. ☐
  – He must have come home early. ☐

c How many people went on holiday?
  – There must have been at least five. ☐
  – There might have been more than five. ☐
  – There must have been three. ☐

d Where did they stay?
  – They could have stayed on a campsite. ☐
  – They must have stayed in a hotel. ☐
  – They might have stayed with friends. ☐

e What did they do on holiday?
  – They must have taken a lot of photos. ☐
  – They could have been sunbathing. ☐
  – They can't have been skiing. ☐

f What did Bob write?
  – He might have written a letter to his wife. ☐
  – He could have written a letter of complaint to the hotel. ☐
  – He could have written a letter to the tour operator. ☐

g How did they travel?
  – They must have flown. ☐
  – They must have gone by train. ☐
  – They might have hired a car. ☐

h What arrived on the next flight?
  – It could have been Marcia's skis. ☐
  – It must have been Marcia's suitcase. ☐
  – It might have been Marcia's coat. ☐

3 Use some of the ideas in sentences a–h to say what you think happened to Andy and Carl.

Example
Andy and Carl must be friends and they must have been on holiday together. They might...

From *New Headway Intermediate* by L & J. Soars (OUP) (reduced). Modal perfects of probability and deduction.

13 Phrasal Verbs

13.1 DEFINITION

A **phrasal verb** is a verb + adverb (e.g. *turn up*). This adverb is often called a **particle**.
A **prepositional verb** is a verb + preposition (e.g. *bank on...*). Prepositional verbs are often called *phrasal verbs* also.
A **three-word phrasal verb** is a verb + adverb + preposition (e.g. *run out of...*).

What these all have in common, and distinguishes phrasal verbs from non-phrasal verbs, is that, to varying extents, their meaning is opaque, or idiomatic, i.e. it cannot be deciphered from the separate parts. *To turn up for the gig* is phrasal; *to turn up your collar* is not.

13.2 ADVERB OR PREPOSITION?

Unfortunately, in many cases the same word can serve as an adverb or preposition, e.g. in [1] *through* is an adverb, but in [2] it is a preposition:
    [1] *The deal fell through.*
    [2] *He fell through the skylight.* (non-phrasal)

Here it is easy to see the difference because the verb is intransitive and the adverb *through* finishes sentence [1], showing up the preposition phrase *through the skylight* in [2]. But in [3] below, the phrasal verb is transitive, obliging it to take an object. This makes the structure appear identical with [4], which has an intransitive verb and a preposition phrase:
    [3] *He gave up the cigarettes.*
    [4] *He walked up the road.* (non-phrasal)

The real preposition phrase can be revealed by **fronting** (moving an item to the front of a sentence):
    [3a] **Up the cigarettes he gave.* [4a] *Up the road he walked.*

Obviously *up the cigarettes* is not a preposition phrase in this instance, and *up* is therefore not a preposition but an adverb.

> **T13.1** | Formulate a rule based on your observation of the following:
> *I put the meeting off.*   *I put it off.*   *I put off the meeting.*   **I put off it.*

come round/come to

From *Making Sense of Phrasal Verbs* by M. Shovel (PH) (reduced). Verb + adverb, intransitive.

14 Questions

1) Become aware of three different types of question by joining the examples with the types below. 2) Only one particular form of one type of question does not require the verb *be* or an aux. verb. Which is this?

EXAMPLE	TYPE OF QUESTION
1. *Are you in Greenpeace?*	a) Wh-question, showing optional object form
2. *Can you smell the lilac?*	b) Wh- question, the wh- word being the subject
3. *Do you like me?*	c) Yes/no question with modal aux. verb
4. *What goes 'zzub zzub'?*	d) Yes/no question with verb *be*
5. *Who(m) can she go with?*	e) Tag question with primary aux. verb
6. *You wouldn't tell, would you?*	f) Yes/no question with primary aux. verb
7. *You liked Sinéad, didn't you?*	g) Tag question with modal aux. verb

Table 14. Question types (task).

Yes/no questions are probably the first type that students acquire, mostly using the verb *be*. As a practice activity a game of '20 questions' or 'What's my job?' can be effective.

Wh- questions even include questions starting with *how*. Teachers ask so many questions that good input is contained in everyday classroom language. For production, songs and information-gap activities such as 'describe and draw' are useful.

Tag questions are perhaps the last type of question that is acquired, being a little difficult in structure and being inessential in communicating facts. Tag questions seek confirmation or agreement, or are used for reproach, humour, etc. The distinction is carried by rising or falling intonation.

Note that **inversion** (the aux. verb or *be* placed before the subject) is a feature of all English direct questions, except when the wh- word is the subject of the sentence (e.g. 4 in the table above).

48.1 *Ask Liz questions. (Look at her answers before you write the questions.)*

1	(where / from?) ...Where are you from?	From London originally.
2	(where / live / now?) Where	In Manchester.
3	(married?)	Yes.
4	(how long / married?)	12 years.
5	(children?)..	Yes, three boys.
6	(how old / they?)...................................	4, 7 and 9.
7	(what / husband / do?)	He's a policeman.
8	(he / enjoy his job?)	Yes, very much.
9	(arrest anyone yesterday?)	
	....	I don't know.
10	(how often / go / on holiday?)	Usually once a year.
11	(where / next year?)	We don't know yet.

LIZ

From *English Grammar in Use* by R. Murphy (CUP). Questions.

15 Clauses

15.1 DEFINITION

When a sentence is itself made up of two or more sentences these sentences are called **clauses**. Clauses are identifiable by their having a verb.

15.2 COORDINATE CLAUSES

When the clauses in a sentence are of equal importance, each having a subject and predicate, they are called **coordinate clauses**. Coordinate clauses are joined by **coordinating conjunctions**, these being mainly *and, or* and *but*, e.g.

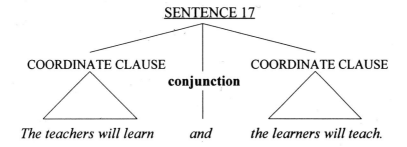

Ellipsis (leaving out a word/words) commonly occurs across coordinate clauses, e.g.
> *The teachers will learn and the learners (will) teach ; I can surf but she can't (surf).*

15.3 SUBORDINATE CLAUSES

When there is a clause which could function as a noun, adjective or adverbial with or within a **main clause**, thus carrying information subordinate to that in the main clause, this clause is called a **subordinate clause**. A **complex sentence** is one composed of a main clause and one or more subordinate clauses.

A subordinate clause often starts with a **subordinator/subordinating conjunction**, e.g.

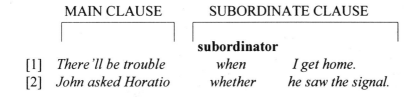

The subordinate clause in [1] is adverbial, and like most time adverbials (here replaceable by the adverb *tomorrow*) can be moved to the front of the sentence or be dispensed with. Not so the subordinate clause in [2], which is a noun clause (replaceable by the noun *something*), the second of two objects required by the verb *ask*.

Observe a subordinate clause in a tree diagram:

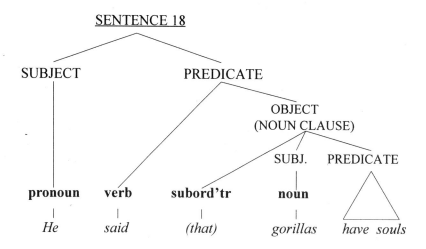

Not all subordinate clauses look as neat as the one in sentence 18 - many have 'invisible' subjects and/or objects, which can be shown 'resurfaced' on the board if such clarification is required.

The following three chapters detail clauses which have become milestones on TEFL syllabuses. These and some others can be introduced as in the table below.

15.4 LIST OF SUBORDINATE CLAUSES

In TEFL clauses are categorized in functional rather than grammatical terms. An exception is participial clauses (not covered here), e.g. *Seeing/Having seen the light : Seen as an imposter*. And perhaps *adjectival* would be more functionally explicit than *relative*. That being said, a list of clauses and their functional types follows.

T15.1 Correctly rearrange the sections in the table below. This is best done, as with most other tasks in this book, by cutting the sections out and matching them.

TYPE	EXAMPLE	SUBORDINATOR
1. REPORTED SPEECH	a) **If I sang out of tune** you would walk out on me.	i) when, before, after, since, while, as, until
2. RELATIVE	b) She sang **as she had never sung before**.	ii) if, unless
3. CONDITIONAL	c) I erected a fence **so as not to be distracted by the topless bathers**.	iii) as (if/though), like, than
4. TIME	d) They said **(that) they wanted peace**.	iv) (that), if, whether
5. PURPOSE	e) I haven't seen him **since he blew three grand at Epsom**.	v) who, that, which, where, whose
6. MANNER/ COMPARATIVE	f) The hand **that rocks the cradle** rules the world.	vi) (in order) to, so (that), so as to

Table 15. Subordinate clauses (task).

16 Reported Speech

16.1 DEFINITION

Traditionally, reported speech (also called *indirect speech*) has always been explained as 'taking the quote marks away'. This still suffices for lower levels, but it would be as well to remember that much 'reported' speech never existed in a 'direct' form, or cannot reveal the direct form. For instance, what were the spoken words in *She told/advised me to leave the vicinity*? They could have been *'You'd better leave now, darling'*, or *'Get lost'*, etc.

Reported *thought* is also understood to be included under reported speech.

16.2 REPORTED STATEMENTS - BACK SHIFT

In reported statements the subordinate clause following the reporting verb has the form of a noun clause. We can call this subordinate clause a reported speech clause.

A typical rule covered by coursebooks is: 'when the reporting verb in the main clause is in the past tense, **back-shift** occurs, i.e. the verb in the reported speech clause changes from present to past, present perfect to past perfect, or past to past perfect as the case requires'. But of course this rule need not always apply:

DIRECT SPEECH	REPORTED/INDIRECT SPEECH
[1] *'I'll be there at eight.'*	She said (that) she'd/she'll be here at eight.
[2] *'I've seen better.'*	She commented that she had/has seen better.
[3] *'I saw Nessie last year.'*	He told me (that) he had seen/saw the monster the previous year.

Table 16. Reported speech - statements.

In [1], if the time of the reporting is still before eight o'clock, *She said she'll be here* is equally acceptable, though *would* can be used to imply some mistrust. After eight, however, only *would* is acceptable. [2] is similarly flexible. In [3] the past simple is an alternative where ambiguity would not arise .

16.3 REPORTED QUESTIONS

In forming most direct questions subject-operator inversion occurs in the subordinate clause, i.e. the (first) auxiliary verb or *to be* is moved from post-subject to pre-subject position. When the question is reported, however, affirmative word order is restored.

16.3.1 Reported wh- questions

DIRECT SPEECH	REPORTED SPEECH
'Where have all the flowers gone?'	She wants to know where all the flowers have gone.
'Where have all the flowers gone?'	She asked me/wondered/wanted to know where all the flowers had gone.

There is a growing tendency to accept the direct question form in spoken reported speech, especially in the case of short questions with the verb *be*. However, it may not be wise to teach these as yet:

She asked me what size was the shirt. : She asked me what size the shirt was.

16.3.2 Reported yes/no questions

To report a yes/no question, *if* or *whether* is used. *Whether* seems preferable when there is more of an aspect of choice. *Or not* may be inserted immediately after *whether* or at the end of the clause beginning with *if* or *whether*.

DIRECT SPEECH	REPORTED SPEECH
?	I was wondering whether (or not)° you would take the bait (or not)°.
'Are you hanging up your stockings?'	She asked (me) if I was hanging up my stockings (or not).

16.4 REPORTED COMMANDS, ADVICE, REQUESTS

Reported commands, advice, requests, etc, generally use the infinitive, e.g.

DIRECT SPEECH	REPORTED SPEECH
'Play the bagpipes.'	She ordered/told/advised/persuaded/asked us to play the bagpipes.

N.B. The caveat of not overdoing grammatical transformations is worth reiterating here. Exercises where students are asked to change a text or a list of sentences from one grammatical form to another (e.g. from direct to indirect speech and vice versa) are rarely seen in coursebooks now, thankfully. Apart from the requirements of a news reporter, etc, much direct and reported speech is better left in its original form.

2 🔊 What happened?

Listen to the sounds on the cassette and write down what *was happening* (past continuous) when something else *happened* (past simple). Make notes first with the help of the words below. Then write a complete sentence. There is an example first.

Example: thumb
He was hammering in a nail when he hit his thumb.

1 joke	6 knock over
2 cut off	7 hiccup
3 sneeze	8 run out of
4 snore	9 ceiling
5 TV	10 shower

3 Grammar practice

Find verbs to complete the following sentences using the past simple (for example, *went*), the past continuous (for example, *was going*) or the past perfect (for example, *had gone*).

Example:
1 ... going to the airport by taxi when I suddenly ... that I ... forgotten my passport.

I was going to the airport by taxi when I suddenly realized that I had forgotten my passport.

1 We ... television when my cousin ... to tell us she ... £100,000 on the football pools.
2 The concert ... when we ... , but luckily our friends ... outside with our tickets.
3 When the journalist ... the scene of the accident, an ambulance ... the injured people to hospital. A police officer ... an eye witness.
4 I ... home late last night. My mother ... to bed, but my father ... in the sitting room.
5 We ... in the garden when the fire alarm ... off. We ... a pan on the cooker and it ...

4 What did he say?

Paola is telling Regina what Richard, an English boy she met, said to her last night. Read the first part and continue Paola's story.

'What's your name?'
'Where are you from?'
'How long have you been in England?'

Well, he asked me what my name was and where I was from. Then he asked how long I had been in England.

'How old are you?'
'Do you want a drink?'
'Are you studying or working?'

When we stopped dancing he ....

....

....

'Where are you staying?'
'Can I see you again?'
'Have you seen the new Michael Jackson film?'

Later he ....

....

....

5 Tell a story

a Form three or four groups. The teacher writes this sentence on the board: 'And that's why I can never forget the name Kathy.'

b The teacher then starts the story by saying, 'It was a dark and stormy night. Outside it was pouring with rain, and I was sitting alone in front of the fire. Suddenly I heard a scream . . .'

c The groups now continue the story in any way they like. One student at a time adds one sentence to the story until it finishes with the sentence on the board. A 'secretary' makes notes of the group's story. Each student thinks of three sentences.

d The secretary of each group tells the rest of the class the story his/her group thought of.

Grammar summary: page 83

From *OK4* by D. Bolton et al (OUP) (reduced). Revising past tenses and reported questions.

17 Relative Clauses

There are mainly two types of relative clause, **identifying** and **non-identifying**. Some grammars use the term *defining* or *restrictive* instead of *identifying*.

17.1 IDENTIFYING RELATIVE CLAUSE

THINGS	1. The boat *that leaves at nine* carries the mail. 2. The piano *which sounds best* was owned by Chopin.	
	3. The boat *whose sails are ripped* will be last.	
	4. The boat *I row* won't cross no ocean.	
	5. The tower *where Strongbow married Aoife* is now a museum.	
PEOPLE	6. The women *who appealed the judge's decision* were brave. 7. There's the hunk *that lit your fire*.	
	8. The woman *whose son is a lexicographer* would like a word.	
	9. The guy *you hired* has been identified as a relative.	

Table 17. Identifying relative clauses (task).

T17.1 Put the letters of the rules below into the corresponding cells in the right hand column of the table above. Some letters will go in more than one cell.

a) The relative pronouns *who* or *that* can refer back to people (*that* sounds a little less respectful).
b) The relative adverbs *where* and *when* are often preferred over *in which, on which*.
c) The possessive relative determiner can refer back to people or things.
d) The relative pronouns *that* or *which* can refer back to things (*which* sounds more formal).
e) If the referent is in the object case in the relative clause then the relative pronoun may be deleted.

17.2 NON-IDENTIFYING RELATIVE CLAUSE

Unlike identifying relative clauses, non-identifying relative clauses are not essential for an understanding of the sentence, as the antecedent in the main clause needs no identifying - it is either [1] a proper noun (name of a person, place or thing) or [2] known to the interlocuters:

[1] *Roberto Calvi, **who was known as 'God's banker'**, was found hanged in London.*
[2] *... and then someone stole his bike, **which you only fixed last week**.*

T17.2 Fill in the blanks:

> A non-identifying relative clause is set off from the (a)_____ clause by
> a comma/commas; in speech, a pause and change in (b)_____ are
> used. Compare with identifying relative clauses.
>
> The relative pronoun (c)'_____' is not used in non-identifying clauses.

Watch your words

Here are eight simple sentences. But can you guess what the words in italics mean?

1 'Oh Charles,' she sobbed. 'They say you're an *embezzler*.'
  a someone who snores
  b a man who has more than one wife
  c someone who steals money from the company they work for

2 'Don't touch that *toadstool*,' he warned.
  a a frog whose bite is poisonous
  b a sharp-edged tool that is used for cutting stone
  c a mushroom that you can't eat

3 'I spent three years in that *orphanage*,' he said, 'and I hated every moment.'
  a accommodation for people whose houses have been destroyed in war
  b a home for children whose parents have died
  c a prison for young people who have committed serious crimes

4 'I've had enough of this *drudgery*!' she screamed.
  a work that is difficult and boring to do
  b food that has a very plain taste
  c conversations that are really about nothing

5 'Over the years,' he said, 'that *couch* has had some very strange people on it.'
  a a bed you lie on while visiting a psychiatrist
  b a table you lie on while having an operation
  c a chair you sit on while having dental treatment

6 'Nobody seems to use *thimbles* these days,' she said.
  a stone bottles you fill with hot water and place in your bed
  b metal cups you wear on your finger while sewing
  c scissors you use to trim the hairs in your nose

7 We spent the afternoon playing *tag*.
  a a children's game in which one player has to try to touch the others
  b a card game in which players try to be first to get rid of all their cards
  c a party game in which players pin cards on each other's backs

8 'Don't go there in August,' she advised. 'There are *midges* everywhere!'
  a young boys who pick people's pockets and snatch handbags
  b badly behaved tourists who spoil other people's holidays
  c small flying insects that bite

Add relative pronouns to these definitions where necessary. Use the quiz answers to help you.

a A bouncer is a person .... throws troublemakers out of nightclubs.
b Slush is snow .... has started to melt.
c A colleague is someone .... you work with.
d Slippers are soft shoes .... you wear indoors.
e A widow is a woman .... husband has died.
f A crèche is a place .... parents can leave small children while they are at work.

From *Language in Use - Upper Intermediate* by Doff & Jones (CUP). Identifying relative clauses.

18 Conditionals

Although we have referred to conditional *clauses* in chapter 15, it is better here to take the term *conditional* to refer to any sentence with an *if* clause and a main or result clause.

For TEFL purposes there are three types of conditional sentence, called, clinically enough, 1st, 2nd and 3rd conditional.

Sentences with *if* which do not fit into the patterns of the 1st, 2nd or 3rd conditional may be called zero or simple conditionals.

18.1 THE FIRST CONDITIONAL

The verb in the *if* clause is in the present tense, the verb in the result clause is in the future tense (or preceded by *might*), e.g.

[1] *If you **study** this book, you **will** have a good grounding in grammar.*
[2] *We'll/we **might** go to the cinema if it **rains**.*
[3] *If it **should** (happen to) rain, we'll go to the cinema.*

T18.1 Fill in the blanks. The numbers refer to the examples above.

1,2. A common error is **If you (a)_____ study this book*. You should point out that English does not use a future tense in a subordinate *if* or time clause as well as in the (b)_____ clause (exception: *If you will please take your seats ...* , where there is an aspect of willingness or invitation - but to avoid confusion don't introduce this till later). Apart from this, students have little difficulty in mastering the first conditional.

2. Regarding punctuation, the (c)_____ is optional when the (d)_____ clause comes first. Otherwise, inserted in this example it would signal an afterthought.

3. *Should* and/or *happen to* is sometimes inserted in the *if* clause to convey that the probability of the occurrence is (e) sl_____. *Should* may begin the sentence when a more formal (f) r_____ is required, e.g. *Should it (happen to) rain ...* .

1-3. The 1st conditional is often given the functional/time title (g)f_____ *conditional*. It could also be called the *quite probable conditional*. In any event these terms should only be used when required, for example, when comparing 1st and 2nd conditionals, which again may not be a communicatively valuable exercise, but is sometimes done for exam preparation.

18.2 THE SECOND CONDITIONAL

The verb in the *if* clause is in the past tense form, the verb in the result clause is preceded by *would* or *could*, or *might*, e.g.

[1] *If I **were** you, I **would** recommend this book to my friends.*
[2] *If Elvis **were/was** alive, he'**d** gyrate in his grave.*
[3] *I'**d** buy a helicopter if I **had** a million dollars.*
[4] *What **would** you do if you **won** the lottery?*

T18.2 Fill in the blanks. The numbers refer to the examples above:

1. Instead of *was* after the 1st (a)_____ singular, *were* is widely preferred. This is an indication that we are dealing not strictly with the past tense in these *if* clauses but the (b)sub_____ mood, used in many languages for unreal events. Note also that for many BrE speakers (c)_____ is often used instead of *would* in this type of sentence.

2. With the 3rd person singular, (d)_____ is more colloquial than (e)_____ .

3. This is a typical example of the use of the 2nd conditional for situations which, for most people, are (f)_____ .

4. This is a typical example of the use of the 2nd conditional for highly (g)im_____ events.

---

1 Look at the pictures. Put the words under each picture in the right order to complete the sentences.

a I usually get the bus to school, but ...

get I if up late lift me Dad gives a my

if _____

b I've got my driving test next week, and ...

pass I test the if buy I'll car a new

if _____

c I don't have any money at all, but ...

million won I a if
round I'd the pounds
travel world

if _____

_____

2 Which situation ... is always true?
... expresses a future possibility?
... is possible but improbable?

PRESENTATION (1)

First conditional and time clauses

1 **T.53a** Jim is going to fly to Istanbul, and then he's going to backpack around the world with his friend, Anthony. His mother is very worried! Listen to their conversation. Put the words from the box in the gaps.

| will you do | won't get | 'll be | 'll get |
| 'll ask | won't do | get | 'll be |

Mum Oh, dear! I hope everything will be all right. You've never been abroad before.

Jim Don't worry, Mum. I _____ OK. I can look after myself. Anyway, I _____ with Anthony. We _____ anything stupid.

Mum But what _____ if you run out of money?

Jim We _____ a job of course!

Mum Oh. What about if you get lost?

Jim Mum! If we _____ lost, we _____ someone the way, but we _____ lost because we know where we're going!

Mum Oh. All right. But what if ...?

Practise the dialogue in pairs.

From *New Headway Intermediate* by L. & J. Soars (OUP) (reduced). 1st conditional (with introduction to 2nd).

18.2.1 Notes on the 2nd conditional

(a) Degrees of probability

The 2nd conditional is used for (a) unreal events (all except example [4] above) and (b) highly improbable events (example [4]). N.B. Don't confuse example [4] with an event of reasonable probability, this being carried by the 1st conditional, e.g. *What **will** you do if you **win** the raffle?* This reveals an area of overlap between 1st and 2nd conditional involving degree of probability and subjectivity.

(b) Functional title

If we were to look for a functional title for the 2nd conditional it might be the *present/future unreal* or *highly improbable conditional*, but many teachers find that the title *imagined conditional* does the trick.

(c) Conditional 'tense'

Some grammars categorize clauses containing *would* as having a conditional *tense*. This may cause confusion, so during the early stages at least, confine *conditional* to sentences and call *would* simply *would*.

18.3 THE THIRD CONDITIONAL

The verb in the *if* clause is in the past perfect tense, the verb in the result clause is preceded by *would have* (or *could/might have*), e.g.

> If I **had known** you were coming, I **would have** baked a cake.

Functionally, this is the 'what might have been' conditional, commonly called the *past conditional*. Both clauses refer to past time. Look out for difficulties with *If I had had...* (primary aux. + main verb).

A combination of 3rd and 2nd conditional is possible, where one clause refers to the present, e.g.

> If I **had taken** his advice I **wouldn't** be in this mess now.

1 Look at the remarks above. What are the speakers talking about?
   What happened (or didn't happen)?

2 Write *If ...* sentences based on the remarks below.

18.4 THE 'ZERO' CONDITIONAL

Structures with *if* which don't fit into the 1st, 2nd or 3rd conditional may be called zero or simple conditionals. There are three main functional types, examples of which follow:

[1] *If you see Olive tell her I need more spinach.*
[2] *If we had money we went to the movies.*
[3] *If it's Tuesday it's Paris.*

T18.3   Match the examples of the zero conditionals above with their functional types below.

> a) TIME CONDITIONAL, the *if* being replaceable with *when(ever)*.
> b) LOGIC, i.e. *If X, then it follows that Y.*
> c) IMPERATIVE.

Because the meanings of the zero conditionals are so transparent and there are no complicated grammatical rules involved in their formation, students have little difficulty in learning them.

18.5 NATIVE SPEAKER 'ERRORS'

There is an inserted *a* in the 3rd conditional in many spoken dialects, e.g.

> *If (only) you had-a stuck at the piano lessons ...*

which may be analogous with the *a* substituted for *have* in the modal perfect, e.g.

> *I could-a strangled him.*

And there are speakers who rarely use the past perfect form in the 3rd conditional:

> *If only you stuck at the piano lessons ...   If I knew then ... ,* etc.

18.6 AMERICAN ENGLISH

Many AmE speakers use *would (have)* in the *if* clauses in the 2nd and 3rd conditional, e.g.

> *If you **would have** persisted, you **would have** gotten through.*

This usage may become globally acceptable in time, so it's questionable whether we should correct a student of English as an International Language on production of such as the above. For the moment, however, it is advisable to present only the orthodox pattern.

18.7 THE SUBJUNCTIVE MOOD

The *were* in *If I **were** you* is said to be a relic of the **past subjunctive** in English, and for all other verbs in similar structures the 'hypothetical past' is used, e.g. *If I **won** a million pounds; If only I **had** a million pounds; I wish you **didn't** smoke so much; It's time we **went** home; As if I **cared**.* This hypothetical past is sometimes also called the past subjunctive.

The **present subjunctive** has the form of the bare infinitive and is used in *that-* clauses after 'suggest/recommend' type verbs. There is an optional *should*, e.g.

> *The board recommends/ed that the accounts (should) **be** checked.*
> *She insists/ed that I (should) **call** the cops.*

It is also to be found in some formulaic expressions, e.g.

> ***Be** that as it may; **Suffice** it to say,* etc.

19 The Infinitive and *-ing* Form

19.1 TERMINOLOGY

We have met the infinitive before (1.4). The infinitive with *to* is the one we refer to here. The term *-ing* **form** is used here to cover *-ing* noun (gerund) and *-ing* participle, because at times it would be difficult and distracting to differentiate between these.

19.2 INFINITIVE AFTER MAIN VERB

An infinitive occurring after the main verb can be an object infinitive or an infinitive of purpose:

> [1] *We began **to play** Pictionary.*   (object)
> [2] *We stopped **to count** the score.* (purpose)

To find out which type the infinitive is, try inserting *in order* before *to*. If there is no great change in meaning it is an infinitive of purpose.

19.3 INFINITIVE OR *-ING* FORM AFTER MAIN VERB

When two verbs come together (without a pause/comma) the second is either an infinitive or an *-ing* form. Depending on the verb(s) and the meaning to be conveyed there may or may not be a choice. **He enjoys to go to the zoo* is a grammatical error. *I won't forget writing* instead of the intended *I won't forget to write* is a semantic one.

19.4 INFINITIVE OF PURPOSE VS. *FOR* + *-ING* OF FUNCTION

Observe:

> [1] **I went to the shop **for buying** some biscuits* ≠ *I went to the shop **to buy** some biscuits.*
> [2] *A spanner is a tool **for turning** nuts.* ≠ *?A spanner is a tool **to turn** nuts.*

Most students, regardless of L1, seem to include pattern [1] in their interlanguage for some time. This is hardly surprising, when we hear *Go to the shop for some biscuits; What did you go to the shop for?* etc.

The solution to this problem is the same as for most others - good examples with enjoyable practice, and if necessary the simple explanation of the rule, here the **purpose/intention of the person (agent) vs. function/use of the instrument.** (Some overlap is possible, of course.)

> **Places to visit for a purpose**
>
> | | | |
> |---|---|---|
> | 1 THE BANK | 8 THE CAPITAL | 15 THE COUNTRY |
> | 2 THE POST OFFICE | 9 A HAIRDRESSER | 16 THE THEATRE |
> | 3 A SUPERMARKET | 10 A CLINIC | 17 A CHEMIST |
> | 4 A HOTEL | 11 A BUS STOP | 18 A TRAVEL AGENT |
> | 5 A SCHOOL | 12 A PUB or BAR | 19 A GARAGE |
> | 6 THE BEACH | 13 A PARK | 20 THE ZOO |
> | 7 THE RIVER | 14 A GYM | 21 A SWIMMING POOL |

From *Grammar Practice Activities* by P. Ur (CUP). Practising the infinitive of purpose.
Adaptation: Student A says 'We would go there to see the sights.' Student B guesses the place. Etc.

Infinitive and gerund 3

verbs taking either infinitive or gerund

A   Tricia works as a diplomat for the Irish government. She has lived in many foreign countries and enjoys her work very much. Her husband, Jim, has always travelled with her, but now he is getting tired of travelling. Tricia has just been offered a new post overseas. Use the verbs to complete what Tricia and Jim say. One of the verbs uses the -ing form and one the infinitive with to each time.

Tricia	Jim	
Example:		
I really enjoy _travelling_ .	I'd prefer not _to travel_ any more.	TRAVEL
1 There are still many places I'd love _____ .	I just don't feel like _____ any more new places.	SEE
2 I love _____ home in different places.	I really don't intend _____ home in any more countries.	SET UP
3 I know I'd hate always _____ in the same place.	I'd just like _____ in one place from now on.	BE
4 I'd miss _____ different ways of life.	I want _____ more about life in Ireland.	EXPERIENCE
5 I hope _____ a lot of money.	I wouldn't mind not _____ a lot of money.	EARN
6 I couldn't stand not _____ anywhere ever again.	I can't promise _____ with Tricia if she takes this job.	GO
7 I can't imagine myself _____ in one place for too long.	I aim _____ in one place, at least for a while.	STAY
8 I've suggested _____ apart for a while.	I've decided _____ apart from Tricia if she wants to travel more.	LIVE

From *Grammar Activities 1* by Forsyth & Lavender (Heinemann). Infinitive or -ing form (gerund) after verbs.

T19.1 Concerning the infinitive and -ing form, which has a 'future' connotation and which implies 'fulfilment'?

20 Negation

20.1 FORM AND USE

To form a negative sentence in English we negate the auxiliary verb or *be*, i.e. we put the negative adverb *not* (often reduced to *n't*), or for emphasis, *never,* after it. If there's no auxiliary verb we insert *do*, e.g.
> *She wouldn't/would never/doesn't dance with hard rockers.*

The contraction can alternate between *be* and the negative adverb, with little if any semantic difference:
> *He's not/He isn't listening.*

Not (and *never*) can also negate other word classes, which involves some ellipsis, e.g.
> *not Josephine, not blue, not running, never on a Sunday.*

20.2 DOUBLE NEGATIVES

Double negatives, e.g. **I didn't see nothing,* are sometimes transferred into English from the student's L1. English doesn't officially allow these but they are popular colloquially, especially in pop songs.

20.3 *NO* AND *NONE*

The negative determiner *no* means *not one/any* before countable, and *not any* before uncountable nouns. It carries a certain emphasis or air of finality:
> *I have no desire to discuss your verrucas.*

None is a pronoun when it stands for *no X*, e.g. *I got none* (no satisfaction).

---

4 Personal problems

should & ought to

She ought not to give him any more pocket money.

She should punish him every time he steals from her.

My son steals

We're an ordinary married couple with two children, an 11-year-old boy and a 4-year-old girl. Two years ago, my son started to steal from me. If I catch him, he cries a lot and promises never to do it again. I don't think he's unhappy: we get on well as a family, and we all do things together in the evenings and at weekends. We give him plenty of pocket money, too. I just can't understand why he keeps on stealing.

She shouldn't leave money lying around the house.

She ought to ask the boy's doctor for help.

She shouldn't punish him – she should try to find out why he steals.

1 Do you agree with any of the advice in the bubbles?

2 Now choose one of these problems, and say what you think the person should do.

From *Language in Use - Pre-intermediate* by Doff & Jones (CUP). Affirmative and negative of *should* and *ought to.*

21 Discourse Markers

21.1 DEFINITION AND WORD CLASS

Discourse markers are cohesive devices, used mainly 1) to relate one sentence (or clause) to another, and 2) to signal the speaker's/writer's attitude or style. They are also called *linkers,* and recently, *signposts.* Without discourse markers we just have bare sentences, no discourse.

Discourse markers are adverbials (see 8.1), sometimes even clauses. They have more to do with vocabulary than grammar. However (did you notice that one?), an introduction here is useful for reference purposes.

T21.1 Match the selection of discourse markers below with their general uses/types.

DISCOURSE MARKER	TYPE
1. *on the other hand*	a) enumerative
2. *then*	b) concessive - reasoning
3. *unfortunately*	c) stylistic - truthful, dismissive
4. *after all*	d) attitudinal - opinion
5. *first*	e) alternative/contrastive
6. *frankly*	f) cause, result, discovery
7. *so*	g) sequential

Table 18. Discourse markers (task).

21.2 OTHER ROLES

Some words that serve as discourse markers may also serve as [1] conjunctions when they join clauses, or [2] adverbs (non-sentential) - in this example the adverb modifies an adjective:
[1] *Ripley was afraid of the phone, so he didn't use it.*
[2] ***however** stressful the work may be.*

21.3 PUNCTUATION

Generally, a comma is usually used to separate the discourse marker from the rest of the sentence, but especially in initial position there is some flexibility and if a faster flow of text is required the comma may be omitted, but not at the expense of clarity, of course.

T21.2 Explain the difference in use between the following adverbials:
a) at the end   b) in the end   c) at last

22   The Articles

The articles (*a*, *the* and *zero*) have 3 main areas of reference in English:
        1. Specific   **2. Generic**   **3. Unique**

22.1 SPECIFIC REFERENCE

Specific here means an actual example of the referent, i.e. the thing/person referred to by the word, e.g. in
A dog *was getting ready to mark my wheel* I am referring to an actual, specific dog (indefinite but specific). When I continue with *I yelled at **the dog*** I am still referring to a specific dog, this time the dog **previously mentioned** (definite and specific). Sometimes the knowledge of the referent can go back some time, or is just **assumed from the context**, e.g. *We went on holidays... we took **the dog** with us.* Forward reference can also apply, e.g. ***the doggy*** *in the window*.

For uncountable and plural nouns the indefinite specific marker is zero or unstressed *some*, e.g.
    She has (some) marijuana/hedgehogs in her garden.

22.2 GENERIC REFERENCE

This is the term covering reference to a class/substance/quality rather than a specific person or thing, e.g.
  A lion *can be dangerous.*   ***The lion*** *is the king of the jungle.*   ***ØLions*** *can be dangerous.*
                                                                           ØHonesty *is the best policy.*

22.3 UNIQUE REFERENCE

22.3.1 Proper names
Names specify what is unique, so they don't require an article, but there are exceptions, especially with postmodification:
    The London *she saw...* ***The Robert*** *she had known*

Some names have a built-in definite article, e.g. *The Hague, The Bronx, The Vatican,* etc.

22.3.2 Community unique
The sun is unique enough for us, but not for astronomers or beings from other galaxies. When *the* is used with *parliament* the interlocuters are usually referring to the parliament in their country. Similarly but again in a smaller community with *the doctor, the grocer's*, etc, and smaller still until we blend with the specific reference assumed from context, as in 22.1 above.

22.4 OTHER USES OF THE DEFINITE ARTICLE

With **comparatives and superlatives**, e.g.
    The faster of the two... the fastest
With **adjectives as nouns**, e.g.
    The rich, the handicapped, etc.

22.5 ZERO OR *THE* IN FIXED PHRASES

    [1] *in hospital/prison - in the hospital/prison*   [2] *to/at work, church; in bed; at home,* etc.
The zero article in [1] connotes a stay rather than pure location; American English prefers the definite article for both uses, though. The zero article in [2] seems similarly to connote state more than location. *Work* meaning place of work always takes the zero article and is preceded by a preposition or *leave*, etc.

23 Recognition Test

T23.1 Match the bold parts of the sentences in the left column with their grammatical labels in the right column. Be careful - there are some redundant labels.

1. He **took over** when John was ill.	a) past participle
2. She couldn't stop **worrying**.	b) infinitive
3. **I'd think twice if I were you**.	c) adverb of degree
4. Where has he **gone**?	d) adverb of frequency
5. You can drive, **can't you**?	e) adverbial
6. Would you like **to dance**?	f) phrasal verb
7. Mine is still trotting after **yours**.	g) tag question
8. I don't know if I **do**.	h) -ing noun (gerund)
9. The meeting**'s been postponed**.	i) -ing participle
10. He played his hand **like a pro**.	j) ellipsis
11. The dog was chasing **its** tail.	k) first conditional
12. The show was **poorly** attended.	l) second conditional
13. The cat was licking **itself**.	m) third conditional
14. It **had been done** before.	n) reflexive pronoun
15. **If I'd known that I would've stayed**.	o) possessive pronoun - independent
16. **'Seen** my student anywhere?	p) possessive pronoun - adjectival
17. Are you **talking** to me?	q) primary auxiliary verb
18. Don't go **unless** you're sure.	r) modal auxiliary verb
	s) past perfect, passive
	t) definite article
	u) present perfect, passive
	v) subordinator

T23.2 Instructions as for **T23.1** above.

19. Demand just dropped **off**.	a) time clause
20. Clarke teed off **after the rain stopped**.	b) demonstrative adjective
21. That's my eldest sister, **who lives in Goa**.	c) demonstrative pronoun
22. Did Adrian ask you **what you did**?	d) genitive case
23. The bike **he had seen** was a Harley.	e) preposition of direction
24. **These** words make up a sentence.	f) adverb of place
25. You **must have known**.	g) adverb particle
26. We're **home**.	h) present continuous tense
27. Is **this** what you brought me here for?	i) discourse marker
28. **In all honesty** I wouldn't have minded.	j) identifying relative clause
29. **They'll be closing** now.	k) non-identifying relative clause
30. Not enough **fruit** is being eaten.	l) future continuous tense
31. It was **the most sensible** thing to do.	m) subject complement (adjective)
32. They didn't have **enough** cop-on.	n) quantifier
33. So **we're leaving** tomorrow.	o) superlative adjective phrase
34. She crashed her **father's** car.	p) reported wh-question
35. James is **unwell**.	q) reported yes/no question
36. She **rose** through the ranks.	r) modal perfect
	s) uncountable noun
	t) collective noun
	u) classifying adjective
	v) intransitive verb

24 Error Analysis

24.1 WHAT WE MUST KNOW ABOUT ERRORS

A full analysis of student errors usually requires investigation of the causes of these, and is usually followed by suggestions for remedial teaching. Concerning the causes, many teachers, even without linguistic training or a command of the student's L1, can see or find out when an error is due to direct translation or overgeneralization of a known rule. More difficult to detect may be overteaching of one form to the detriment of another, cross-cultural problems, avoidance strategies, etc.

The proportion of errors caused by L1 interference can range from about 30% to 65%, depending on the student's L1, i.e. the more the L1 resembles English the more the student will be inclined to use the syntax and lexis of their language, often falling into the trap of using what are known as 'false friends' in the process.

In language learning, errors are to a great extent manifestations of the student's progress along the learning path. Also keep in mind that some students like to experiment, making inevitable errors, while others prefer to wait until they are confident that what they produce will be correct.

On a point of terminology, the word *mistakes* in this field is reserved for slips of the pen or tongue, i.e. anything the student will self-correct if it is pointed out. *Errors*, on the other hand, are not readily recognised as such by their producers. In this chapter we also understand an error to be 1) spoken, 2) not part of the objective of the lesson in which it occurs, and 3) not above the production level of the student.

24.2 CORRECTING ERRORS

It is as well to state here that many teachers do not believe in correcting. In truth there is not enough conclusive research evidence to allow prescriptive methods in this regard. Furthermore we each have our own way of correcting people when we are in conversation, and carry a preferred method into the classroom. On the part of the student, and this is the priority of course, again you will find mixed attitudes, but perhaps leaning towards more rather than less correction.

Leaving that aside, in your ELT training course you may be asked to design an on-the-spot error-correction technique, usually for a spoken error, small class, and presuming the other students would appreciate the mini-lesson also. A suggested procedure would be to follow a shortened version of the popular (and often criticized) *three P's* model (presentation, controlled **practice**, free **practice**). Due to the descriptive detail involved in the following example its execution would seem to take some time, but actually no more than five or ten minutes is recommended to be spent on this.

ERROR: **I no like cabbage.*

DESCRIPTION OF ERROR: The rule for the formation of negative statements from affirmative ones which have no auxiliary verb and whose main verb is not *be* is: after the subject insert the auxiliary *do* (present tense) followed by the negative adverb *not*. These are usually contracted to *don't* (for third person singular read *does ... doesn't*). The student has not applied this rule.

CAUSE OF ERROR: usually taken to be L1 interference, e.g. from Spanish:
> *No me gusta el repollo.*

CORRECTION:

Presentation:

1. Thank the student for her contribution and 'soft correct' with, e.g. *So, you don't like cabbage, Cristina. What about potatoes? And potato crisps? ... you know,* (say popular brand name) *munch, munch? ... Ah, too much salt, yes. You know what I don't like? ... I don't like garlic. Ugh. I hate it. Onions are okay, but I don't like garlic* (draw garlic or translate if monolingual class). Cristina should have registered awareness of the error and correct form by now.

2a. Write the correct version on the board. Say the sentence at almost normal speed. Underline or otherwise highlight the relevant parts: *Cristina doesn't like cabbage.* Under that add *I don't like garlic* (the 'I' on a board should only refer to the writer, as much as possible). Elicit and re-read while writing.

2b. Beside each sentence after writing, include a drawing to aid memory and add enjoyment. This allows further input, e.g. *Now here's Cristina, pointing to some cabbage. She really doesn't like cabbage. No, sir!* Note: don't be afraid to draw - even if your attempts are awful it's always fun and encourages participation. Chat and elicit vocab, spelling, etc, from students while drawing.

2c. Elicit another example for the board from a student. *What about sports, hobbies? Juan, do you like fishing?* If Juan just says 'No' or 'Yes' accept this. *Ah, so you like fishing, that's nice. I'm afraid I don't; I fall asleep. What about football, tennis, skiing?* Now Juan cannot just say 'no' or 'yes'. Write the third model sentence on the board, with a drawing. This can be positive rather than negative, for comparison: *Juan likes fishing.*

Figure 4. Board for presentation of *Don't like*.

Controlled practice:

Controlled practice is generally understood to mean repetition in one form or another, with 'hard' correction. We all know that children are great mimics, and when we are learning a troublesome phrase in a new language we repeat the phrase, usually to ourselves, to get the 'feel' of it. What happens in the class, though, for this stage largely depends on the students. Some nationalities and age groups love 'sing-song' repetition; others would think it strange to be asked to repeat a sentence just for the sake of getting used to it. For these latter, controlled practice usually means intensive T-S (teacher to student) question and answer sessions and/or intensive controlled pair work. On average, though, a young class would repeat a model sentence twice without becoming bored, so we'll presume such a class. Of course, if pronunciation and rhythm are ok little or no repetition is necessary.

Model (pronounce clearly with an indication for repetition) *She doesn't like cabbage,* indicating stress pattern by gesturing with your hand/finger or tapping on the desk/board. Ask students to repeat, following your gesture - it is important that they keep together, and this cannot be done without your 'conducting'. If they enjoy this choral repetition ask for another repetition, 'hard correcting' where appropriate (hard correction is where you point out that an error has been made, clearly repeat the model again and ask for another effort). Finally, ask for individual repetition of one of the students, to check. Accept any decent effort and move on.

Do likewise with the second sentence on the board, changing the 'I' to your name (drilling should never be meaningless).

Elicit a different like/dislike sentence to add variety, and treat in the same way. Try to remain a little conversational throughout this and other stages, commenting on food, sports, politics in a not too detailed way: *Whiskey? Yes, I like whiskey at night, then I don't like whiskey in the morning, ouch (ha ha). Now listen and repeat...* etc.

Free practice:

Free practice generally means students genuinely conversing with each other without interruption from the teacher. If there's time for preparation, cards, pictures or other aids can be organised for information gap or information sharing activities, but as this error correction is taken to be carried out 'on-the-spot' the teacher only has the board and classroom furniture as materials and generally uses relevant topics and language generated by the students themselves. Pair work is usually the best grouping for this stage.

1. Ask students to get into pairs.
2. Specify about 3 topics and write them on the board, e.g. *food, sports, animals.* Elicit more topics for choice. Tell students they must write down at least one answer for questions on each topic.
3. Student A asks two questions (*What food do you like? What food do you not like?*) and writes down at least one answer given by student B. The answer sentence could contain two clauses if the students are capable, e.g. *Fidel likes carrots but he doesn't like peas.* Then it's B's turn to ask.
4. The pairwork should be demonstrated by the teacher with a good student before letting the whole class commence the activity.
5. When more than half of the students have finished, stop the pair work.
6. Ask for a few sentences and write them on the board. Comment briefly and thank all students. This part is important because it reassures the students that there was a reason for writing down the answers, and it can provide some communal fun to round off.

Alternative pairwork:
1. Students write down, without showing their neighbour, what they like and don't like - topics on the board.
2. Student A asks student B to guess the liked/disliked item, within 3 guesses. Clues should be given. Score a point if student B can't guess. Then alternate.
3. As points 4 to 6 above, but also ask about and comment on some scores.

Role-play as an alternative to question-and-answer pairwork:
1. Allot roles and scenarios that would elicit *like* and *don't like.* Students can help you with this, often being quite imaginative. One suggestion would be a careers interview with a candidate that's not too keen on what's on offer; or mother and teenage daughter in a clothing store, the mother trying to buy 'sensible' clothes for her daughter; or at the dining table, more cajoling of a child who is picky about his food, etc, etc.
2. Demo a short role-play with a good student.
3. Ask pairs to write brief notes rather than a full script for their role-play. Groups of three might also be suitable. Remind students to include *like* and *don't like* in the script, and to keep it short, about three turns each.
4. Some fun can now be had as each pair (or as many as time allows) acts out their script.
5. Check that the correct form has been reinforced and thank all students.

The sentences below contain typical errors made by EFL students. Define the errors accurately, always using grammatical terms. The first one has been done for you.

0. I don't know what will I do.
   No inversion required in reported question.

1. Many people die and many buildings destroy.

   ....

2. We were chatting, then we went downtown for seeing a movie.

   ....

3. He hasn't got some wine.

   ....

   ....

4. There are two kinds of date trees, one growth in the north and one in the south.

   ....

5. How can I to go there?

   ....

6. Claus has come to visit me last week.

   ....

7. Sometimes I'm going to the shops.

   ....

8. There's nothing to do, so I'm very boring.

   ....

9. I want to avoid the mistakes who the teachers made before.

   ....

10. He buyed a new car last year.

    ....

11. She is going to give up to smoke.

    ....

12. The factory closed and a lot of people lost their works.

    ....

13. They need believe in something.

    ....

14. I was walking by a dark street.

    ....

15. We met there a strange woman.

    ....

16. We asked her if she can bring Jim Morrison back to life.

    ....

17. We went back to home.

    ....

18. After a flight of two hours - most of it we spent studying - we landed in Gdansk.

    ....

19. The life is very hard there.

    ....

20. My first reaction was to shout, but after I thought this was not a good idea.

    ....

ANSWERS TO TASKS

T1.1

sloop (noun only)   *rile* (verb only)

T1.2

Transitive: *discover, respect.*   Intransitive: *kneel, prosper.*

T1.3

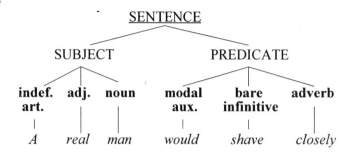

T1.4

Suggested: *The skimpy scissors are discussing cuts.*

T1.5

SENTENCE 7: (a) PREDICATE   (b) **indef.art., modal aux., bare infinitive, adverb**
(c) *An opening would help immensely.*
SENTENCE 8: (a) SUBJECT   (b) OBJECT   (c) **def.art., noun, bare infinitive, def.art., noun**
(d) *The Turkish play might shock the audience.* (For a note on *shall* see 12.2.)

T1.6

1 a) noun b) *-ing* participle   2 a) modal aux. b) def. art.   3 a) aux. b) pronoun
4 a) bare infinitive b) adverb   5 a) pronoun b) adjective

T1.7

A preposition must be followed by a noun/-phrase or pronoun. *To* in *look forward to* is a preposition, evidenced by the noun following it in, for example, *look forward to <u>summer</u>*. A noun is therefore required - in this case an *-ing* noun (gerund) - instead of the infinitive *see*.

T1.8

1 a) aux. verb b) prep.   2 a) noun b) *-ing* noun/gerund   3 a) aux. verb b) pronoun
4 a) linking verb b) adjective (*well* often acts as an adverb, e.g. *He cooks well*)
5 a) def. art. b) *-ing* noun/gerund   6 a) modal aux. b) *-ing* participle   7 a) adverb b) adjective

T1.9

SENTENCE 13: (a) OBJECT   (b) ***-ing* noun/gerund   verb   pro.   prep.   noun**
(c) *Gambling drove him to hell.*
SENTENCE 14: (a) COMPLEMENT   (b) **def. art.   noun   linking verb   adj.**
(c) *The discount sounds good.*

T2.1

1. future continuous   2. present continuous   3. past simple   4. present simple   5. past continuous
6. future simple

T2.2 Please go to bottom of page 68

T2.3

1. future simple   2. present simple   3. present perfect simple   4. present continuous
5. past simple   6. present perfect continuous   7. future continuous   8. past continuous

T2.4

1. future simple   2. past perfect simple   3. present perfect continuous   4. future perfect simple
5. past simple   6. past perfect continuous   7. past continuous   8. present perfect simple
9. present continuous   10. future perfect continuous

T2.5

TENSE	EXAMPLE	USE
1. PRESENT SIMPLE	g) *You just never listen, do you?*	v) regular, habitual
2. PRESENT CONTINUOUS	k) *She's putting up a good fight.*	ix) happening now
3. PAST SIMPLE	e) *Sister Stan made her point.*	xiii) past event (non-concurrent)
4. PAST CONTINUOUS	f) *I was just looking at it.*	xi) concurrent past event
5. FUTURE WITH *GOING TO*	m) *You're not going to watch* Casablanca *again, are you?*	iv) plan/intention
6. FUTURE SIMPLE/ FUTURE WITH *WILL*	a) *It'll be alright on the night.*	vi) prediction (non-concurrent event)
7. FUTURE CONTINUOUS	h) *Bill will be seeing his secretary Monday.*	i) prediction of concurrent event
8. PRESENT PERFECT S.	j) *That's torn it.*	viii) recent event or life experience
9. PRESENT PERFECT C.	i) *How long have you been telling that joke?*	xii) continuous up to now
10. PAST PERFECT S.	c) *The plant had grown a foot in our absence.*	x) event or life experience before main past reference
11. PAST PERFECT C.	b) *We'd been trying to get it started.*	vii) concurrent event before main past reference
12. FUTURE PERFECT S.	l) *They'll have destroyed half the rainforests by 2015.*	ii) predicted to have happened by a future time
13. FUTURE PERFECT C.	d) *They'll have been talking for ten hours come midnight.*	iii) continuous event up to a future time - duration stated

T2.6

1c) 2a) 3e) 4d) 5b)

T2.7

a) state in the past   b) habitual event in the past

T2.8

Any semantic difference there is usually hinges on the connotation of finality with the perfect simple, e.g. in [3] the speaker may well be about to move house. The perfect continuous, on the other hand, is often employed for focussing on duration, and the act is expected to continue.

T3.1

1, 3 a)   2, 4 b)

T7.1

TYPE OF SET	TYPE OF ADJ	EXAMPLES/SET
(a) OPEN	1. qualitative	(iv) *dark, efficient, friendly, wet, sweet, soft* ...
	2. classifying	(iii) *electric, Korean, medical, legal, oak, pregnant* ...
(b) CLOSED	3. demonstrative	(i) *this, that, these* and *those.*
	4. quantitative	(ii) *all, any, another, each, little/a little* ... (total approx. 20, not counting numerals or *of*+ types)

T7.2

1)

	SIZE	QUALITY	COLOUR	NATIONALITY	MATERIAL	PURPOSE	
A	*big*	*old*	*red*	*Victorian*	*ceramic*	*water*	*jug*

2) The macro types *qualitative* and *classifying* could be loosely spread, the former from SIZE to COLOUR and the latter from NATIONALITY to PURPOSE.

T8.1

1c) 2a) 3e) 4b) 5d)

T2.2

Suggested:

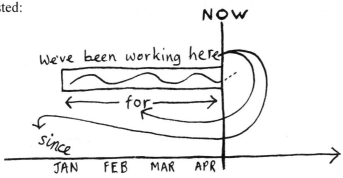

T10.1

TENSE	ACTIVE	PASSIVE
PRESENT SIMPLE	*She draws pictures.*	*Pictures are drawn by her.*
PRESENT CONTINUOUS	*She is drawing fruit.*	*Pics. are being drawn by her.*
PAST SIMPLE	*She drew an alien.*	*An alien was drawn by her.*
PAST CONTINUOUS	*She was drawing wine.*	*Wine was being drawn by her.*
FUTURE SIMPLE	*She'll draw blood.*	*Blood will be drawn by her.*
FUTURE WITH *GOING TO*	*She's going to win the competition.*	*The competition will be won by her.*
FUTURE CONTINUOUS	*She'll be drawing the pension.*	*The pension will be being drawn by her.* [R]
PRESENT PERFECT S.	*She has drawn U2.*	*U2 have/has been drawn by her.*
PRESENT PERFECT C.	*She has been drawing bananas and grapes.*	*Bananas and grapes have been being drawn by her.* [R]
PAST PERFECT S.	*She had drawn more pictures that morning.*	*More pics. had been drawn by her that morning.*
PAST PERFECT C.	*She had been drinking wine.*	*Wine had been being drunk by her.* [R]
FUTURE PERFECT S.	*She will have drawn 100 pictures by next Sunday.*	*100 pics. will have been drawn by her by next Sunday.*
FUTURE PERFECT C.	*She will have been drawing fruit for 7 weeks.*	*Fruit will have been being drawn by her for 7 weeks.* [R]

The [R] signifies that the future continuous and the continuous perfects are very rarely used in the passive.

T11.1
The following, corrected below, were incorrect or incomplete:

2 blow   blew   blown
7 hurt   hurt   hurt
8 lie   lay   lain
9 mow   mowed   mown/mowed

American English reference is *Merriam-Webster's Collegiate Dictionary, 10th edition.*

T13.1
The object of a transitive phrasal verb may go between the verb + adverb or after the verb + adverb, except when the object is a pronoun, when it can only go between the verb + adverb.

T14.1
1): 1d)   2c)   3f)   4b)   5a)   6g)   7e)
2): Wh- question, the wh- word being the subject (example 4).

T15.1

TYPE	EXAMPLE	SUBORDINATOR
1. REPORTED SPEECH	*d) They said **(that) they wanted peace**.*	iv) (that), if, whether
2. RELATIVE	*f) The hand **that rocks the cradle** rules the world.*	v) who, that, which, where, whose
3. CONDITIONAL	*a) **If I sang out of tune** you would walk out on me.*	ii) if, unless
4. TIME	*e) I haven't seen him **since he blew three grand at Epsom.***	i) when, before, after, since, while, as, until
5. PURPOSE	*c) I erected a fence **so as not to be distracted by the topless bathers**.*	vi) (in order) to, so that, so as to
6. MANNER/ COMPARATIVE	*b) She sang **as she had never sung before**.*	iii) as (if/though), like, than

T17.1
1,2 d)   3 and 8 c)   4 and 9 e)   5 b)   6,7 a)

T17.2
a) main   b) intonation   c) *that*

T18.1
a) *will*   b) result/main   c) comma   d) if   e) slight/slim   f) register   g) *future*

T18.2
a) person   b) subjunctive   c) *should*   d) *was*   e) *were*   f) unreal/untrue/impossible
g) improbable

T18.3
[1] c)   [2] a)   [3] b)

T19.1
The infinitive usually carries a future connotation; the *-ing* form usually implies fulfilment.

T21.1

DISCOURSE MARKER	TYPE
1. on the other hand	e) alternative/contrastive
2. then	g) sequential
3. unfortunately	d) attitudinal - opinion
4. after all	b) concessive - reasoning
5. first	a) enumerative
6. frankly	c) stylistic - truthful, dismissive
7. so	f) cause, result, discovery

T21.2

a) *at the end* usually refers to position in a book, race, etc.

b) *in the end* refers to how a story ended, often ironically.

c) *at last* implies some impatience, the awaited being overdue.

T23.1

1 f	2 h	3 l	4 a	5 g	6 b	7 o	8 q	9 u
10 e	11 p	12 c	13 n	14 s	15 m	16 j	17 i	18 v

T23.2

19 g	20 a	21 k	22 p	23 j	24 b	25 r	26 f	27 c
28 i	29 l	30 s	31 o	32 n	33 h	34 d	35 m	36 v

T24.1

(Chapter references follow for most points. In the case of 1.4, the 4 refers to sentence 4 and remarks thereat.)

1. Passive voice required when the object of the action comes first in the sentence (10.1).
2. *For* + -ing form used instead of infinitive of purpose (19.4).
3. *Some* is used in affirmative sentences, *any* in questions and negatives (5.5).
4. Instead of the noun *growth*, the past participle *grown* should be used in this 'elliptical passive' construction (10.2) (15.2).
5. The infinitive without *to* should follow a modal auxiliary (1.4), or modal + subject, in the case of inversion (14).
6. *Start* should be in the past tense, as a past time has been mentioned (2.6).
7. Present simple required for habitual actions (2.1 - table 1).
8. Past participial instead of -ing adjective required, as there is a descriptive vs causal dichotomy with *bore, interest, tire, excite, confuse, amuse,* etc. (7.2).
9. Relative pronoun for things is *that* or *which* (T17.1).
10. Overgeneralisation, treating an irregular verb as regular. Past tense and past participle is *bought* (11).
11. The (phrasal) verb *give up* is transitive and requires a noun/-phrase or -ing form as object (13.2).
12. *Work* can only be used as a count noun to refer to works of art, literature, etc. The count noun required is *job* (4).
13. *Need to* is the correct semi-modal apparently being sought. *Need* as a modal is generally used only in the negative or interrogative (12.6).
14. Wrong choice of preposition. *Along* would be more suitable.
15. Adverbs of place usually go in end position (8.3.2).
16. Back-shift rule should be implemented in reported speech (16.2).
17. *Home* is an adverb of direction in this case, not a noun requiring a preposition of direction (8.2).
18. Relative pronoun *which* required in non-identifying relative clause (17.2).
19. Generic reference with uncountable nouns requires zero article (22.2).
20. *After* usually serves as a preposition, whereas a sequential discourse marker is required here. Choice of *then, later, afterwards, etc,* would be better (21.1).

INDEX

Reference is generally to chapter (and section), sometimes to a task. Reference to chapter 1 is by sentence, e.g. 1.9 is to be read as chapter 1, sentence 9 and remarks thereat.

a indefinite article 1.5, 22
absolutely emphasizer 7.4
able to 12.6
adjective 7, 22.4
adverb 8, 21.2, relative T17.1, negative 20.1, sentence 21.1
adverb particle in phrasal verb 13.1, 13.2
adverbial 1.15, 8.1, 21.1
agent 10.2
agreement 3rd person -*s* 2.1, sex-neutral pronoun 6.5
always adverb of frequency 8.2, 8.3.3
and coordinating conjunction 15.2
antecedent 17.2
any general determiner/quantifier 5.1, *some* and *any* 5.5
anyone indefinite personal pronoun 6.5
apostrophe 6.1
article 1.4, 1.5, 5.1, 22
as if + subjunctive 18.7
aspect 2.3, 2.6
at last, *in the end* and *at the end* T21.2
auxiliary verbs 1.4, 1.5, 2.6.1, 2.6.3, 12, 20.1

back-shift in reported/indirect speech 16.2
be aux verb 1.5, linking verb/copula 1.12, negative contraction 20.1, subjunctive 18.7
better, best 9
but coordinating conjunction 15.2
by + agent in passive voice 10.2

can modal auxiliary verb 1.4, 12.2
case 1.10
clause 15
command imperative 1.1, 1.4
comparative and superlative forms 9, with *the* 22.4
complement 1.12
complex sentence 15.3
conditionals 18
conjunction coordinating 15.2, subordinating 15.3
continuous aspect 2.3
contracted forms 2.7, 2.10, 20.1
could modal auxiliary 12, in conditionals 18.2, 18.3

dare/daren't semi-modal 12.6
determiner 5.1, 20.3
diary future 2.11
discourse marker 21
do primary auxiliary verb 12.1, 20.1
drunken adjective 7.2.2

ellipsis 15.2, 20.1
emphasizer 7.4
error analysis 24
few and *little* 5.4

fronting 8.3.2, 13.2
function 2.2
futures 2.10, 2.11
genitive/possessive case 6.1
gerund 1.11, 19.1
going to future 2.10

hard adjective 7.1, adverb 8.2
hardly negative adverb 5.5
help verbs see auxiliary verbs
home 8.2, 22.5
hospital with zero or definite article 22.5
how many/much 5.2
however discourse marker 21.1, adverb 21.2

if in conditionals 18, in reported speech 16.3.2
if/whether reported questions 16.3.2
if only 18.7
imperative 1.1, 1.4
indirect speech 16
infinitive 1.4, 19
inflexion 2.10, 12.6
-ing **form** 19.1
-ing **noun** 1.11, 19.1
-ing **participial adjective** 7.2.1
-ing **participle** 1.5
intensifier 7.4, 8.3.5
interrogative (question) 14
interested and *interesting* 7.2.2
intonation 14, T17.2
inversion 14, 16.3
its and *it's* 6.1
it's time + subjunctive 18.7

linkers 21.1
little and *few* 5.4
live, work continuous act verbs 2.14
look forward to + *-ing* noun T1.7
lots of and *a lot of* 5.3

many and *much* 5.3
may modal auxiliary 12
modal auxiliary verb 12
modal perfect 12.7
much 5, 8.3.5

need, needn't semi-modal 12.6
negation 20
never frequency adverb 8.2, 8.3.3, negative adverb 20.1
nobody, no one indefinite personal pronoun 6.5
none 20.3
not negative adverb 20.1

noun 4
  -ing 1.11, 19.1
  proper 17.2, 22.3.1
noun phrase 1.10

object 1.1, 1.10, 10.2, 15.3, 17.1
omission of letters see contracted forms
omission of word(s) see ellipsis 15.2
ought to 12.2, 12.5

part of speech 1.10
participle -ing (present) 1.5, 7.2.1, past 2.6.1, 7.2.2,
  10.2
passive 10
perfect aspect 2.6
person 1.9, 6
phrasal verb 13
pluperfect 2.7
postmodification 22.3.1
possessive/genitive case 6.1
predicate 1.1
preposition 1.9, 1.10
prison with zero or definite article 22.5
progressive aspect 2.3
pronoun 1.9, 6

quantifier 5
question 14

rarely 5.5
recommend + *that*- clause 18.7
referent 22.1
register 12.4
relative clause 17
reported speech 16

scissors summation plural 4.2
seem stative verb 2.13
seldom 5.5, 8.3.3
shall 12.2
short forms see contracted forms
should 12.5, 18.1, 18.7
simple and continuous aspects 2.3
since with present perfect T2.2, subordinator 15.4
singular and plural number pronouns 1.9, nouns 4.2
so 15.4, 21.2
some and *any* 5.5
subject 1.1, 1.10, 10.2
subjunctive mood 18.7
subordinator 15.3
suggest/recommend type verbs 18.7
summation plurals 4.2
superlatives 9
syntax 1.15

that demonstrative pronoun 6.4, demonstrative
  adjective 7.1, relative pronoun 17.1
that- clauses 18.7
the definite article 1.4, 22
think stative verb 2.13

this demonstrative pronoun 6.4, demonstrative
  adjective 7.1
through adverb or preposition after verb 13.2
transformation 16.4

used to 2.12, 12.2

verb
  auxiliary 1.4, 1.5, 2.6.1, 2.6.3, 12, 20.1
  continuous act 2.14
  dynamic 2.13
  finite 1.1
  lexical 1.5
  linking 1.12
  main 1.4, 1.5, 2.6.3, 12.1
  modal auxiliary 12
  phrasal 13
  primary auxiliary 12.1
  stative 2.13
  suggest/recommend type 18.7
  transitive 1.2, 1.10, 10.2
verb phrase 1.15
verb tenses 2
very intensifier 7.4, 8.3.5

were subjunctive 18.2, 18.7
whether in reported speech 16.3.2
which relative pronoun 17
who relative pronoun 17, */whom* question word
  T14.1
whose relative pronoun 17
will and *going to* 2.10, and *shall* 12.2, in reported
  speech 16.2, in 1st conditional 18.1
wish + subjunctive 18.7
wonder as reporting verb 16.3.1, 16.3.2
word class 1.10
work 2.14, 4.1.2d, 22.5
worse, *worst* 9
would and *used to* 2.12, modal auxiliary 12, in
  reported speech 16.2, in conditionals 18.2, 18.2.1c,
  18.3

zero article 22
zero conditional 18.4